PIANO • VOCAL • GUITAR

P9-DMJ-852

CONTEMPORARY BROADWAY

BROADWAY

ISBN 0-634-03625-4

HAL•LEONARD®
CORPORATION
7777 W. BLUEMOUND RD. P.O. BOX 13819 MILWAUKEE, WI 53213

Visit Hal Leonard Online at
www.halleonard.com

CONTENTS

ELABORATE LIVES
from Walt Disney Theatrical Productions' AIDA

Music by ELTON JOHN
Lyrics by TIM RICE

Moderately, with rubato

RADAMES:

We all lead such e-lab-o-rate lives

Wild am-bi-tions ___

in ___ our sights ___ How an af-fair ___

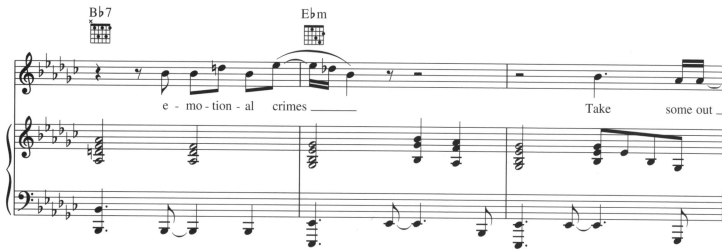

We don't know whose words are true ___

Strang - ers, lov - ers, ___ hus - bands,

wives ___ Hard to know who's lov - ing ___

___ who ___ **AIDA:** Too man - y choic - es tear us a - part ___

WRITTEN IN THE STARS

from Walt Disney Theatrical Productions' AIDA

Music by ELTON JOHN
Lyrics by TIM RICE

think of me or speak of me and won-der what be-fell _____ The

some-one you once loved ___ so long a-go, _____ so well!

RADAMES:

Nev-er won-der what I'll feel _ as liv-ing shuf-fles by _____

You don't have to ask _ me and I need not re-ply _____

A CHANGE IN ME

from Walt Disney's BEAUTY AND THE BEAST: THE BROADWAY MUSICAL

Words by TIM RICE
Music by ALAN MENKEN

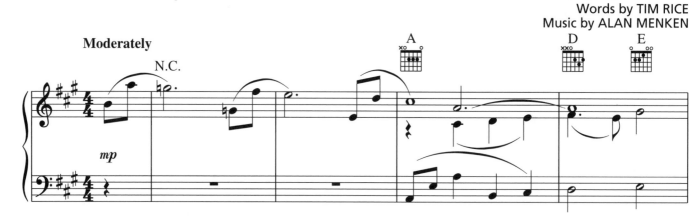

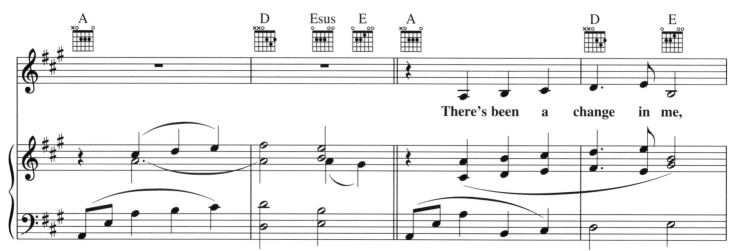

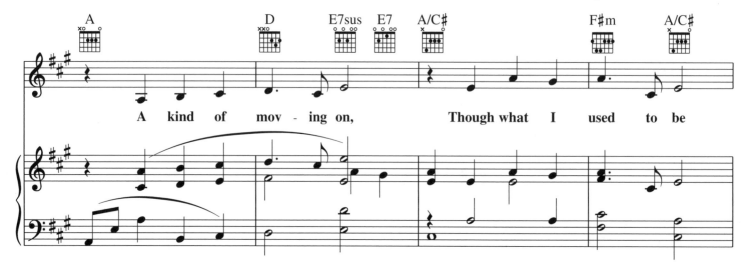

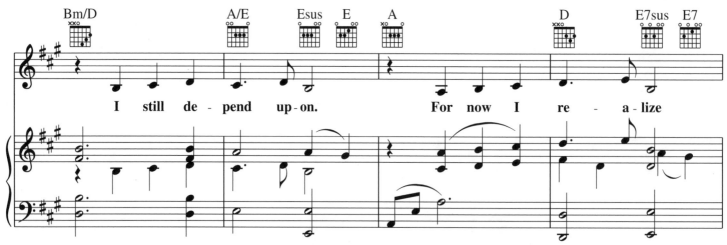

had dis - ap - peared for good, But in its place I feel

a tru - er life be-gin. And it's so good and real,

It must come from with-in. And I, _____

poco rall. *mf a tempo*

I nev - er thought I'd leave be - hind _____

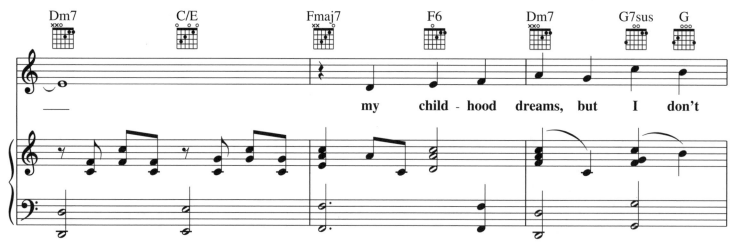

my child - hood dreams, but I don't

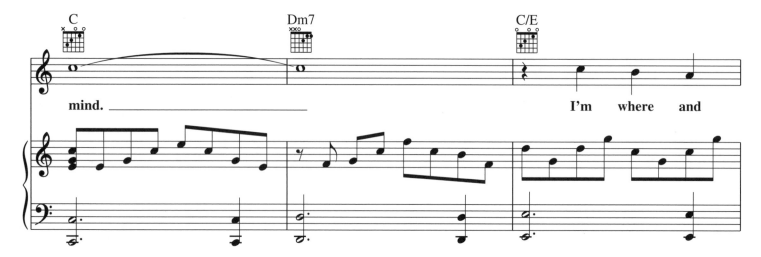

mind. _____ I'm where and

who I want to be. _____

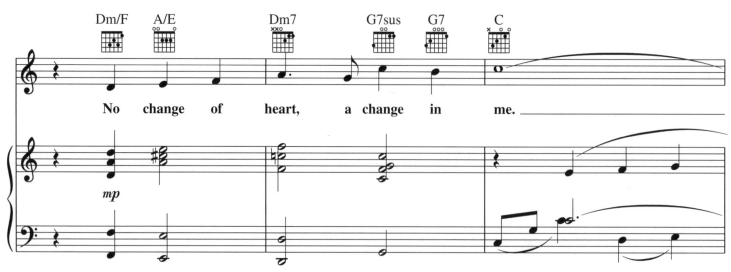

No change of heart, a change in me. _____

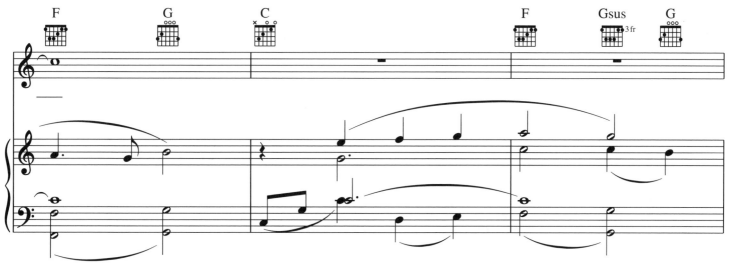

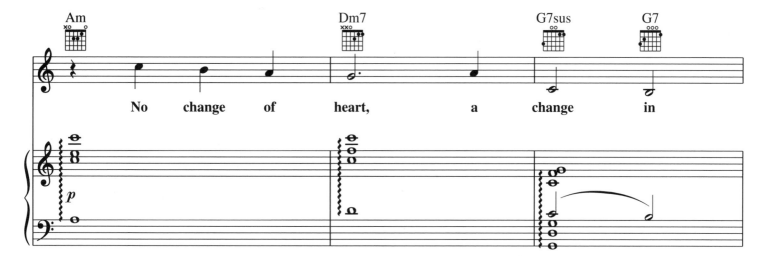

No change of heart, a change in

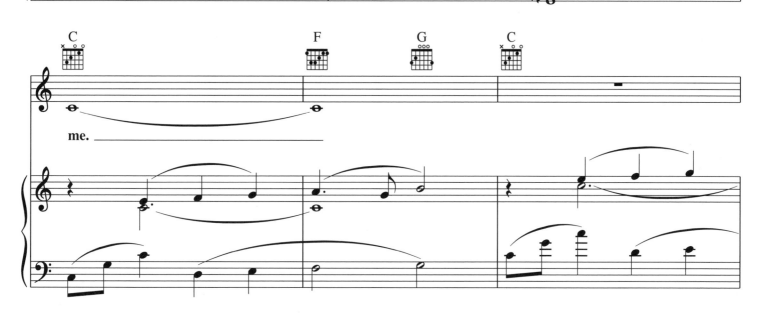

me. _____

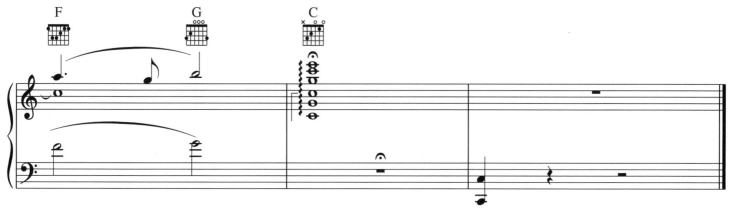

SOMETHING THERE

from Walt Disney's BEAUTY AND THE BEAST: THE BROADWAY MUSICAL

Lyrics by HOWARD ASHMAN
Music by ALAN MENKEN

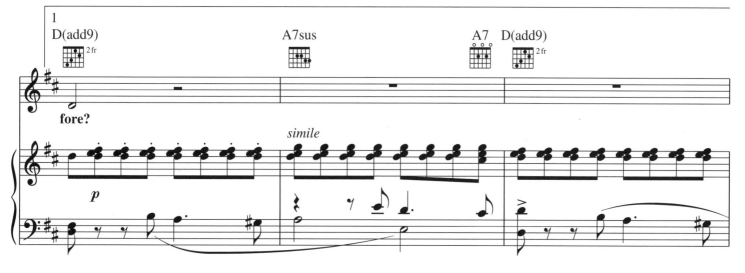

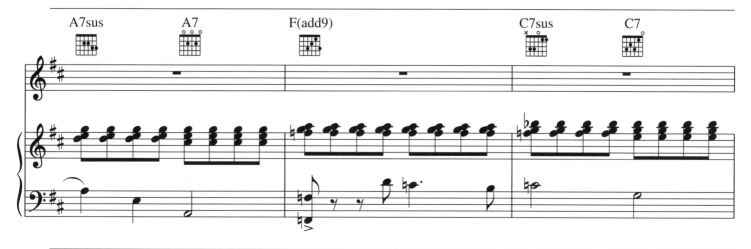

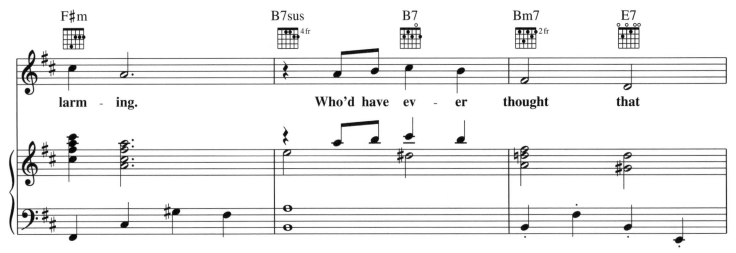

larm - ing. Who'd have ev - er thought that

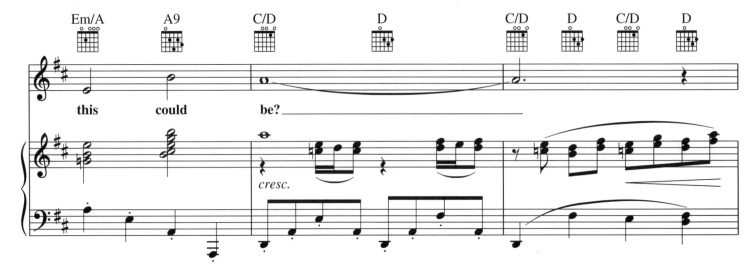

this could be? _____

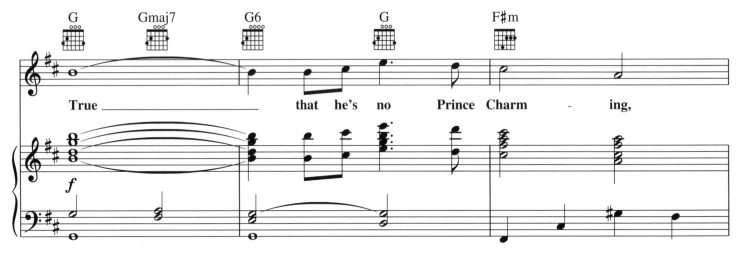

True _____ that he's no Prince Charm - ing,

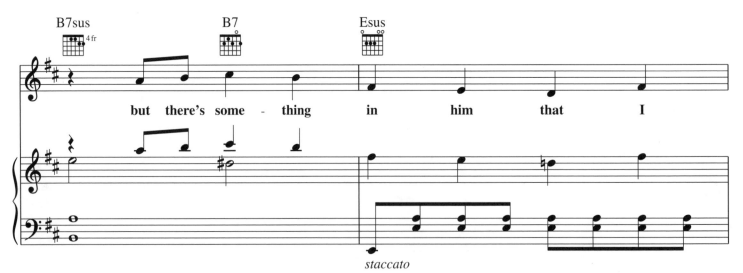

but there's some - thing in him that I

CAN YOU FIND IT IN YOUR HEART?

from the Broadway Musical FOOTLOOSE

Words by DEAN PITCHFORD
Music by TOM SNOW

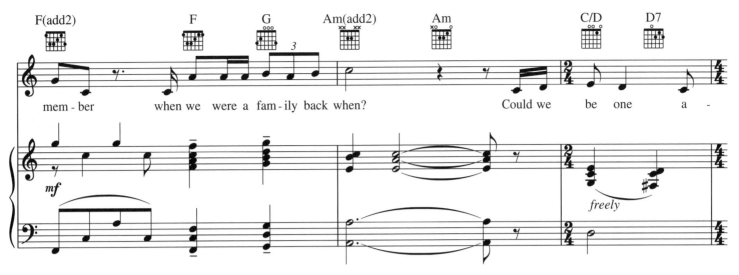

mem - ber when we were a fam-ily back when? Could we be one a -

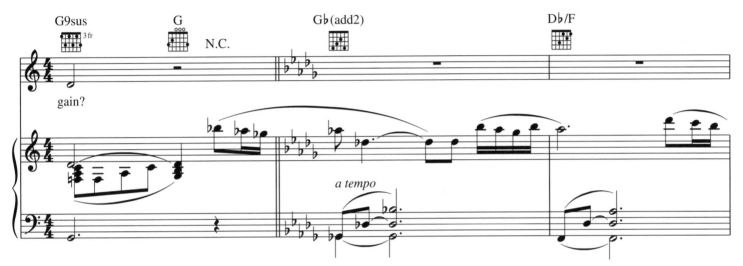

gain?

Does it ev - er cross your mind that I

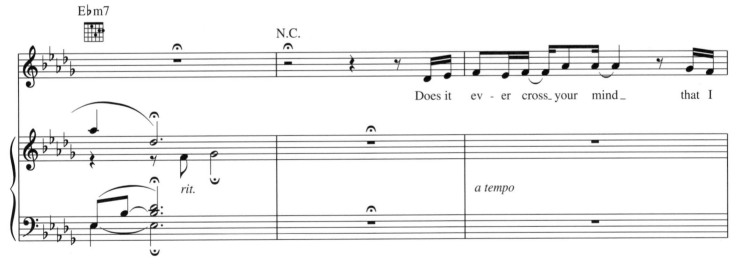

miss you? Is there an - y chance we'll find the joy that we

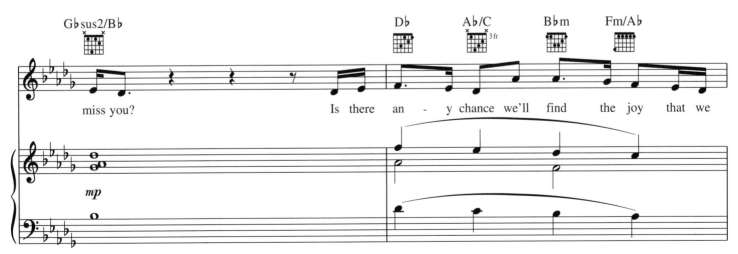

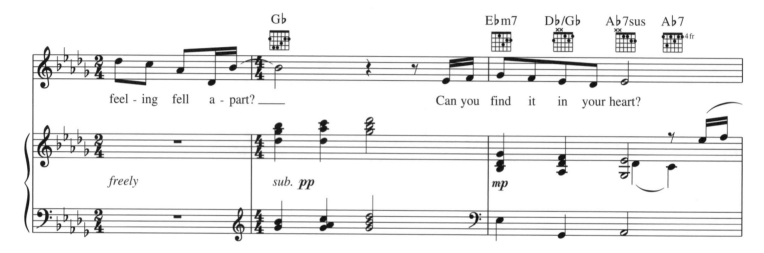

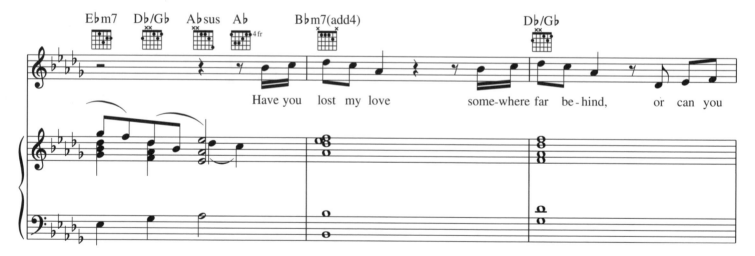

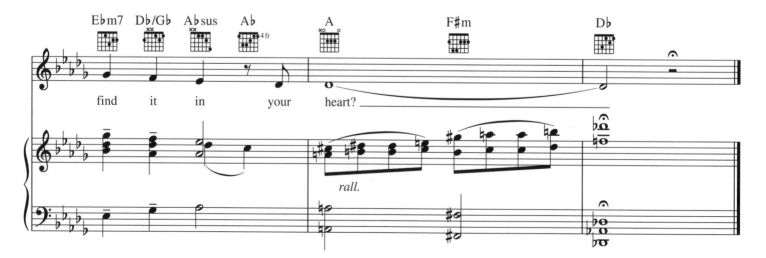

ALMOST PARADISE
from the Broadway Musical FOOTLOOSE

Words by DEAN PITCHFORD
Music by ERIC CARMEN

Moderately Slow Rock Ballad

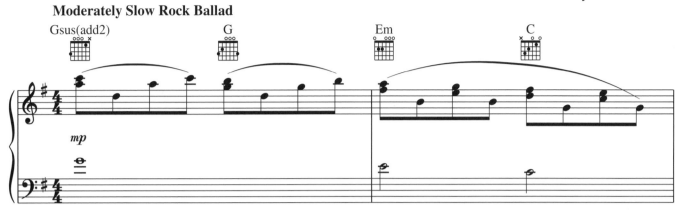

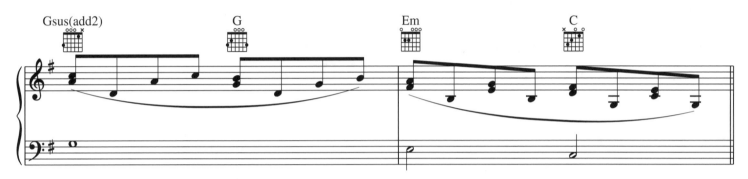

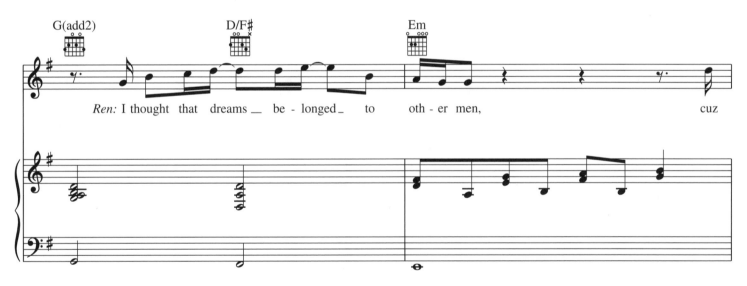

Ren: I thought that dreams __ be- longed __ to oth-er men, cuz

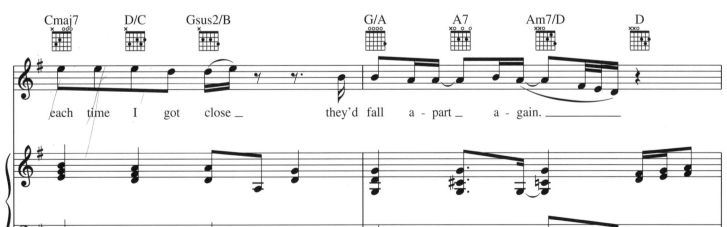

each time I got close __ they'd fall a-part __ a-gain.

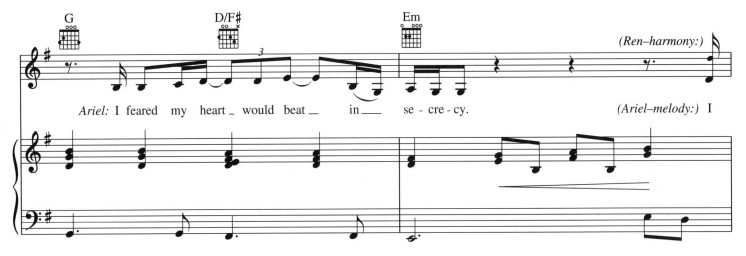

Ariel: I feared my heart would beat in se-cre-cy.

(Ren–harmony:)

(Ariel–melody:) I

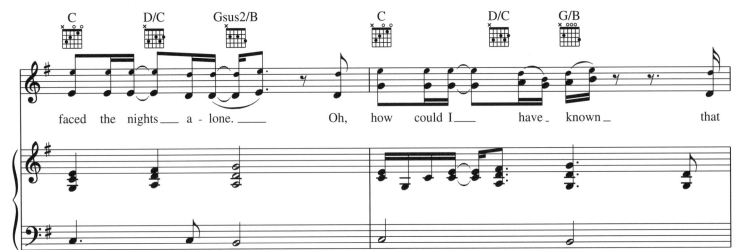

faced the nights a-lone. Oh, how could I have known that

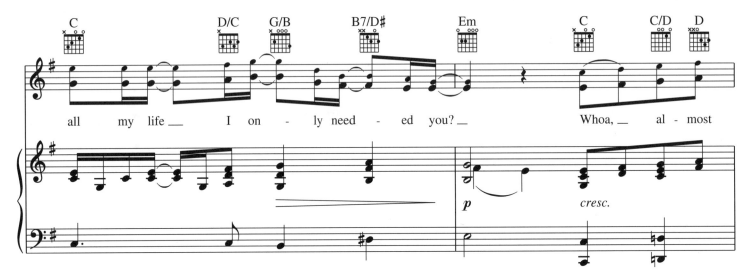

all my life I on-ly need-ed you? Whoa, al-most

par-a-dise, we're knock-ing on heav-en's door. Al-most

par - a - dise; _____ how could we ask_ for _____ more? I

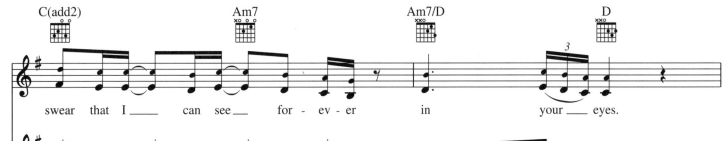

swear that I ____ can see_ for - ev - er in your ___ eyes.

decresc.

Par - a - dise. _

mp

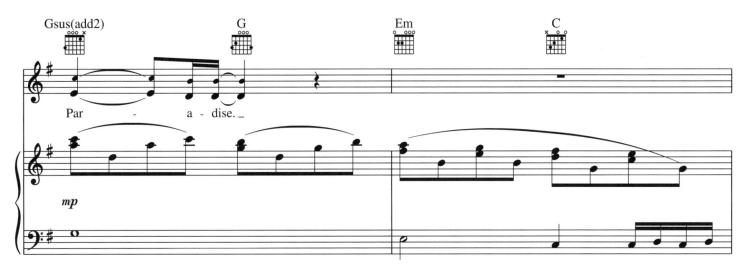

Ariel: I thought that per - fect love _ was hard to find. I'd

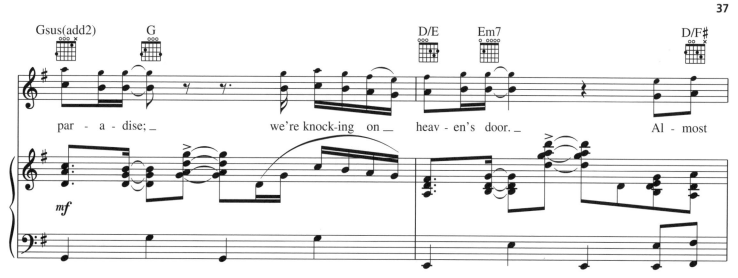

par - a - dise; _ we're knock-ing on _ heav - en's door. _ Al - most

par - a - dise; _ how could we ask _ for _ more? I

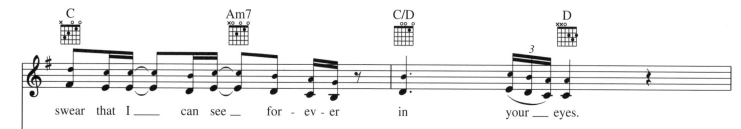

swear that I _ can see _ for - ev - er in your _ eyes.

Par - a - dise. _

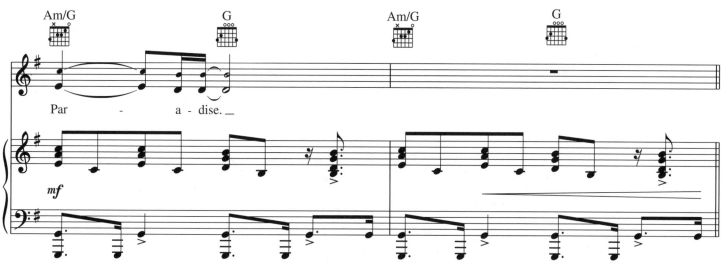

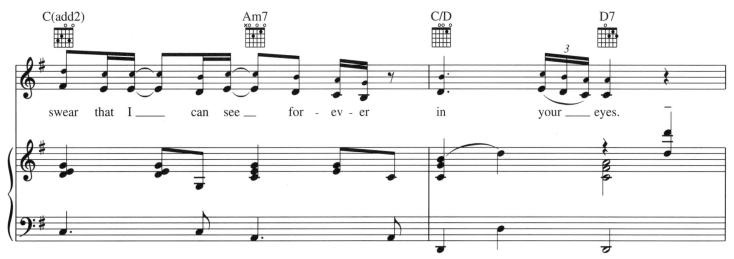

swear that I ___ can see ___ for - ev - er in your ___ eyes.

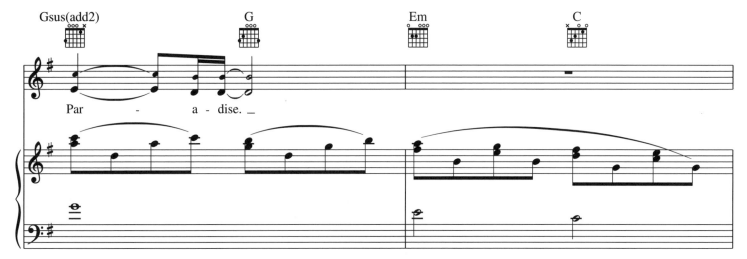

Par - a - dise. ___

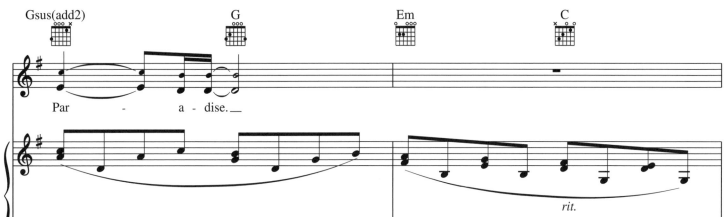

Par - a - dise. ___

Par - a - dise. ___

LIFE IS JUST A BOWL OF CHERRIES

from FOSSE

Words and Music by LEW BROWN
and RAY HENDERSON

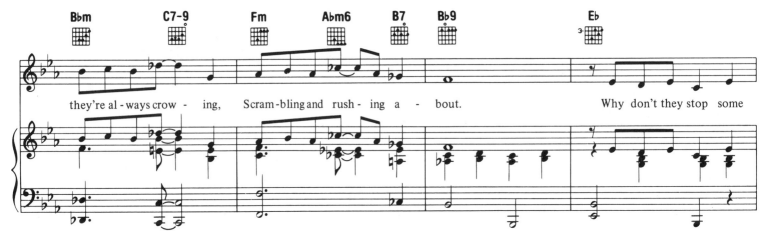

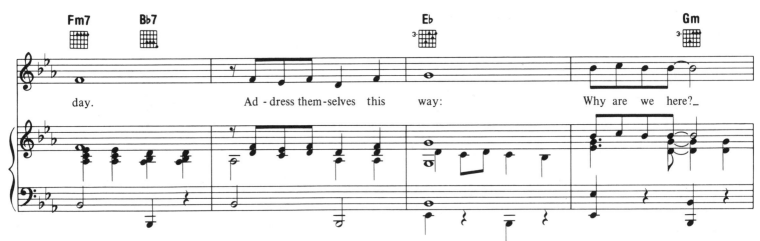

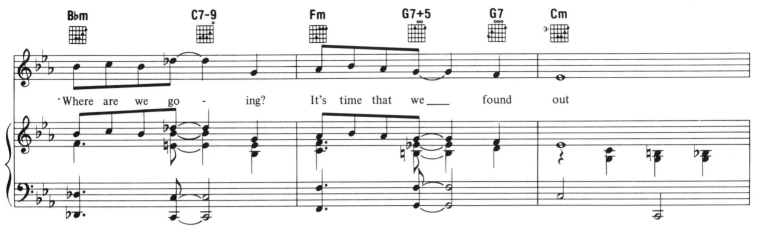

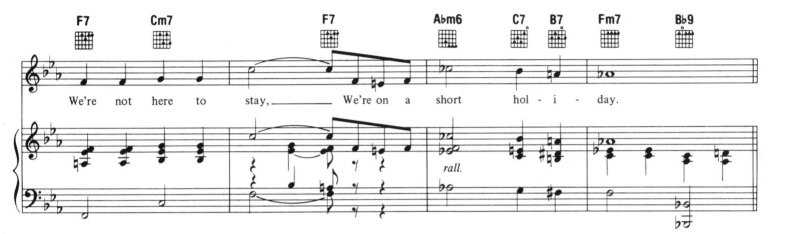

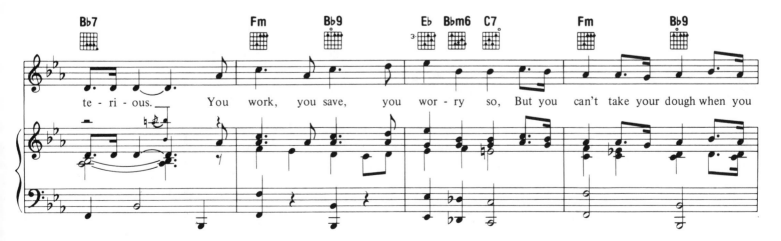

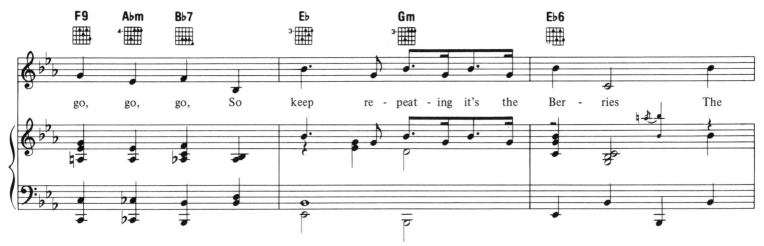

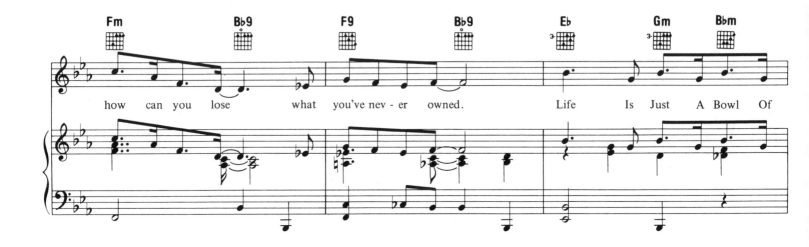

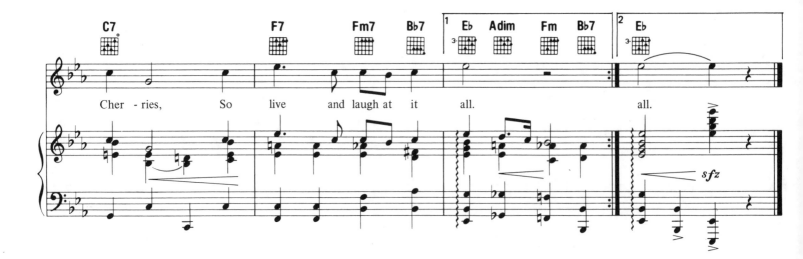

FROM THIS MOMENT ON
from FOSSE

Words and Music by
COLE PORTER

Moderately slow

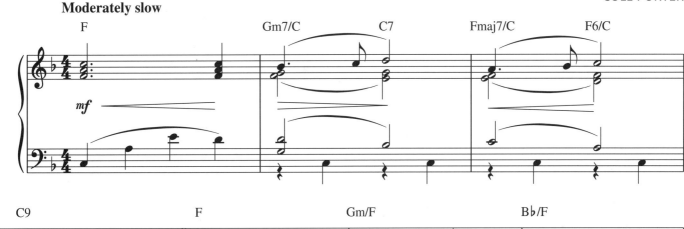

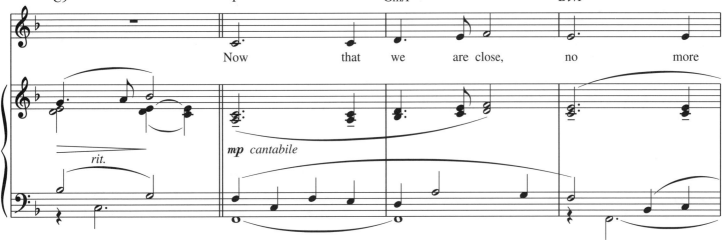

Now that we are close, no more nights mor-ose, Now that we are one, the be-guine has

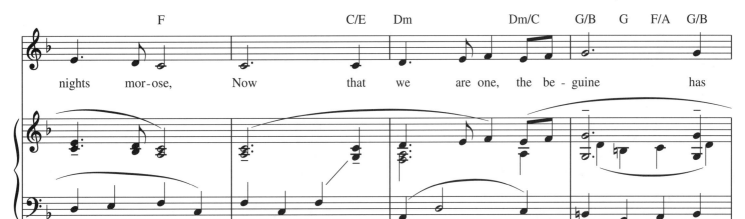

just be-gun. Now that we're side by side,

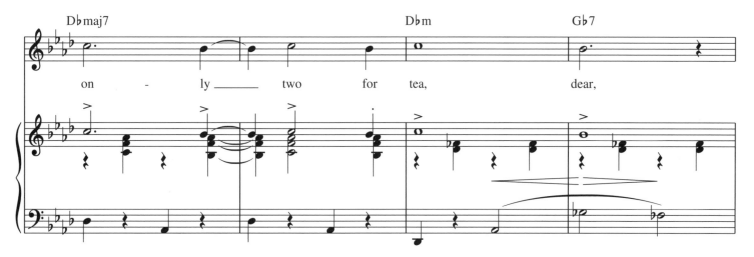

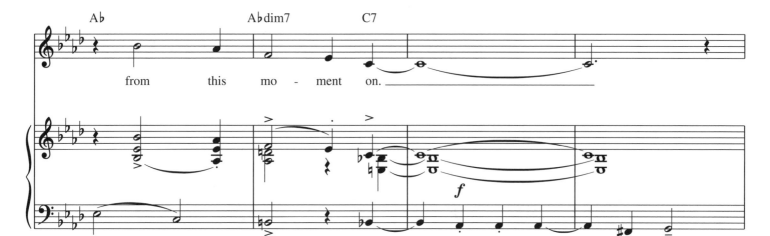

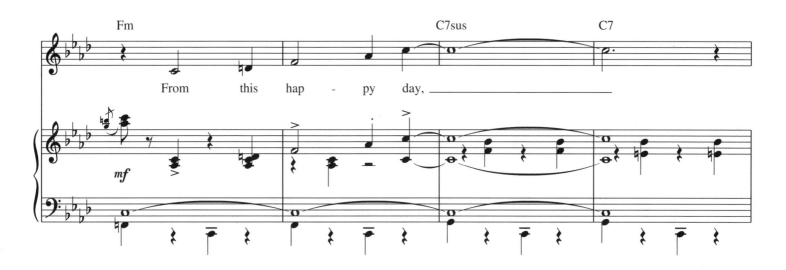

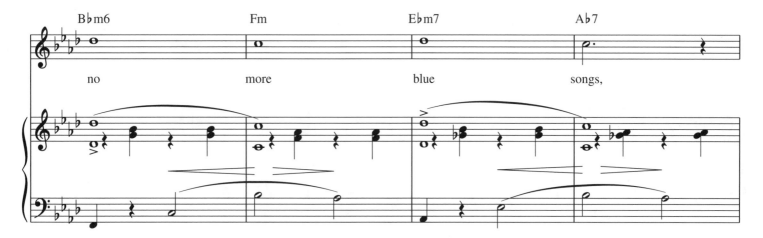

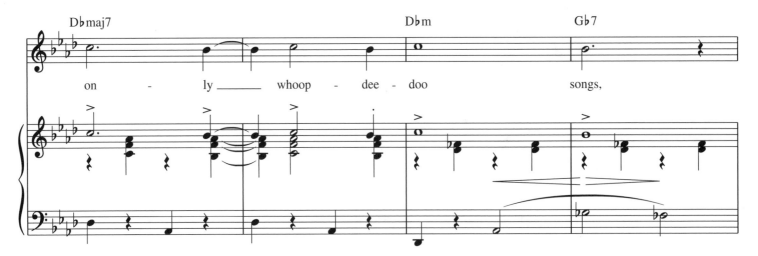

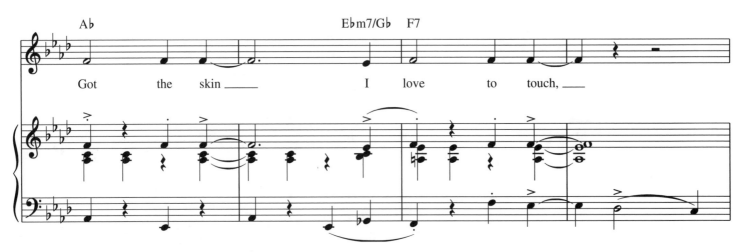

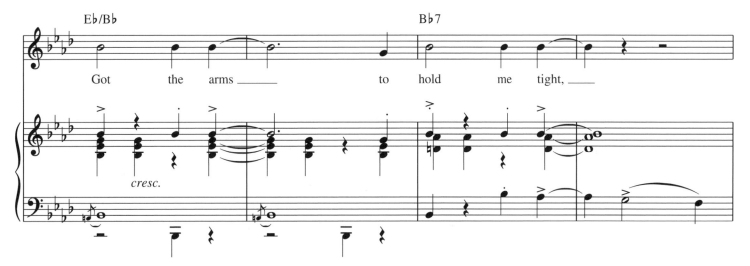

Got the arms _____ to hold me tight, _____

Got the sweet lips _____ to kiss me good-night, _____

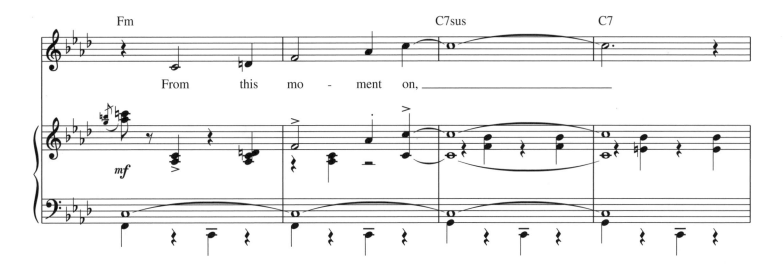

From this mo - ment on, _____

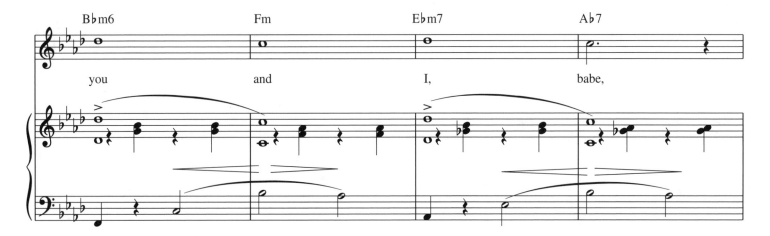

you and I, babe,

48

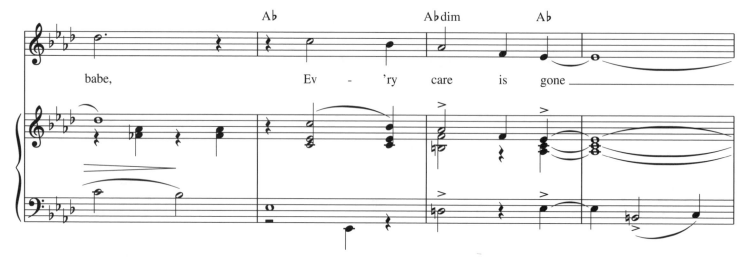

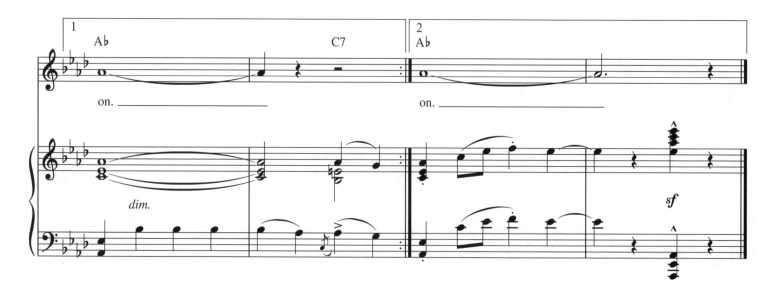

YOU RULE MY WORLD

from THE FULL MONTY

Words and Music by
DAVID YAZBEK

on-ly you.... not feet or knees. You

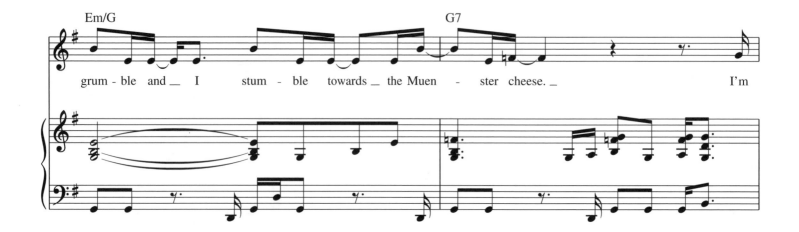

grum-ble and __ I stum-ble towards __ the Muen - ster cheese. __ I'm

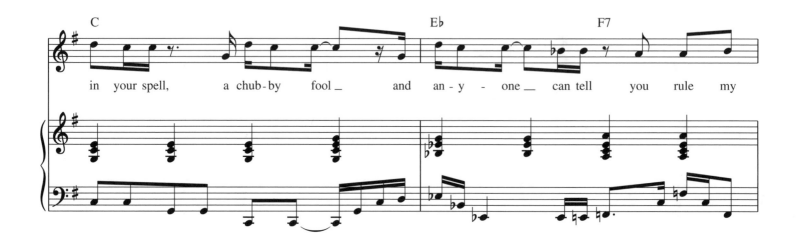

in your spell, a chub-by fool __ and an-y - one __ can tell you rule my

world my world no mat-ter what I do __ you rule my

DAVE: world.

HAROLD: Look at you _____ my life, my dream _ my la-dy with the eight-y dol-lar

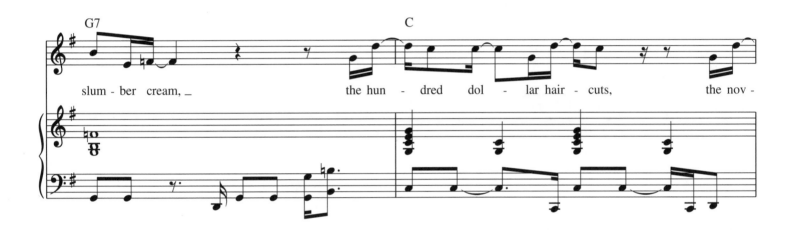

slum-ber cream, _ the hun-dred dol-lar hair-cuts, the nov-

-el-ty _ ap-pli-an-ces _ we nev-er use, _ and all _

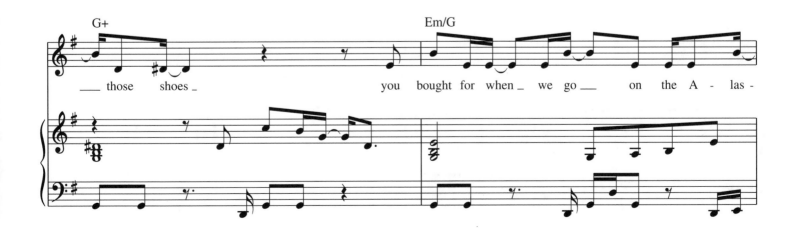

_ those shoes _ you bought for when _ we go _ on the A-las-

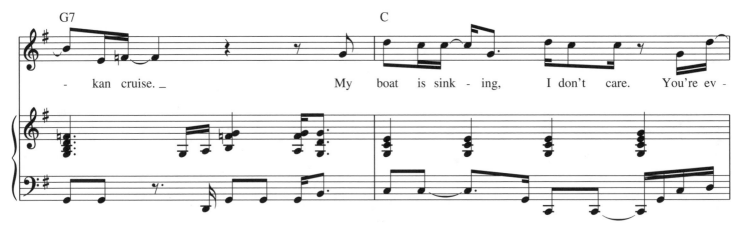

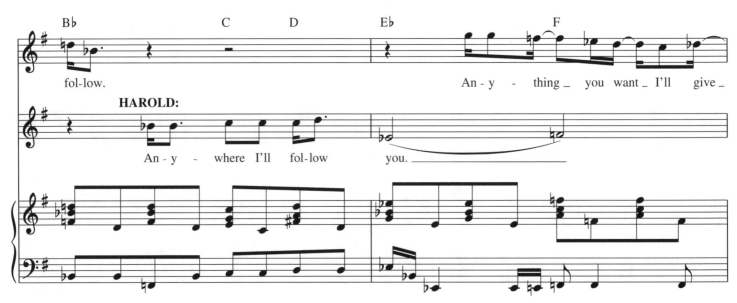

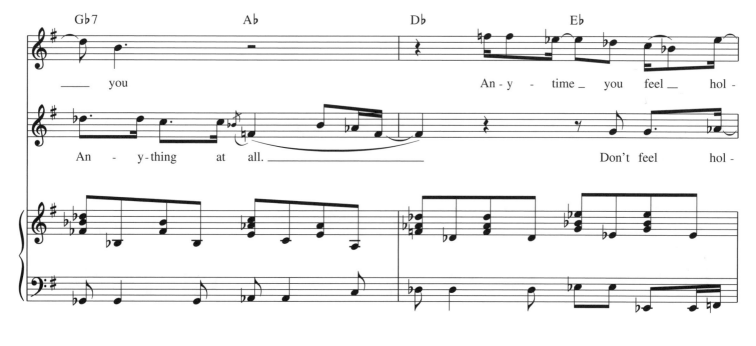

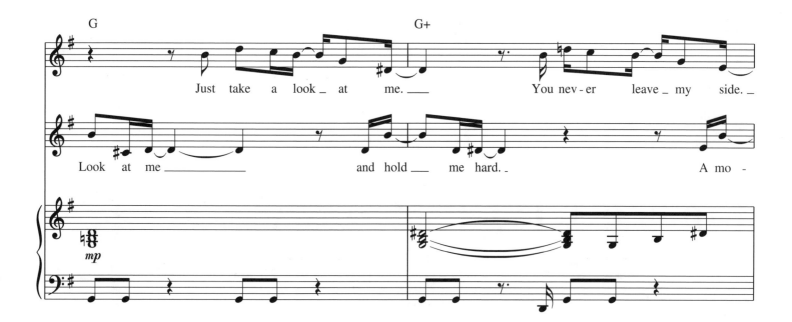

Why can't I let __ you go? __

-ment please, __ be-fore __ they seize the Vi - sa card! __ 'Cause

Why can't I just lose— you rule my

I'd do an - y-thing __ to keep __ you. You rule my

world, my world. Though I'm

world, my world.

DAVE:

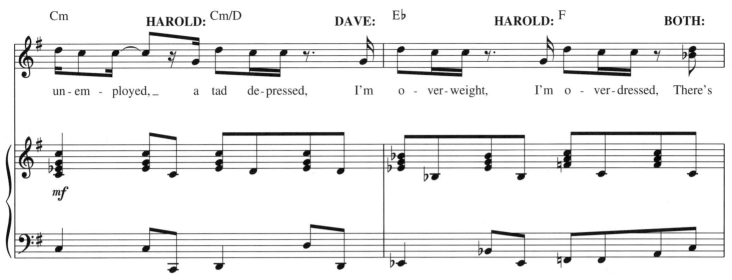

un-em - ployed, _ a tad de-pressed, I'm o - ver-weight, I'm o - ver-dressed, There's

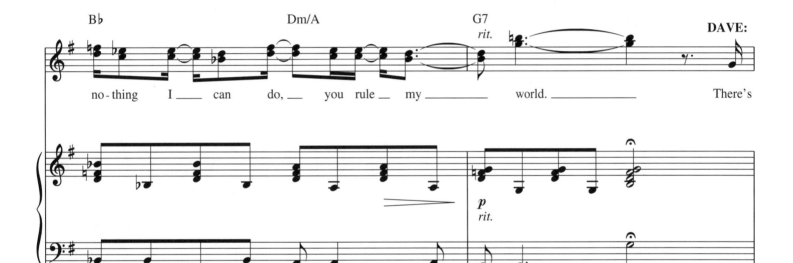

no-thing I __ can do, __ you rule __ my _____ world. _____ There's

Slower

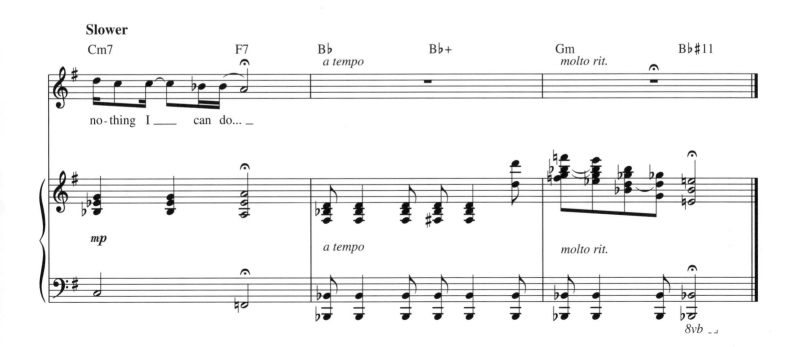

no-thing I ___ can do... _

8vb

YOU WALK WITH ME

from THE FULL MONTY

Words and Music by
DAVID YAZBEK

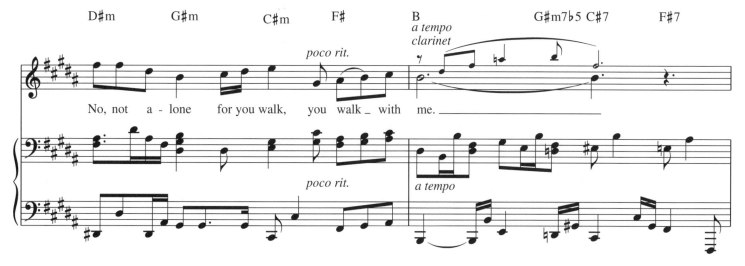

No, not a - lone for you walk, you walk _ with me. _____

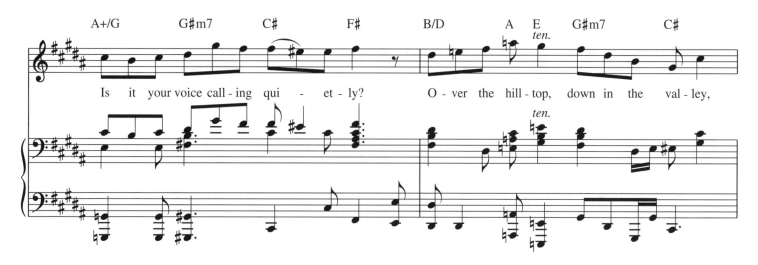

Is it the wind there o - ver my shoul-der?

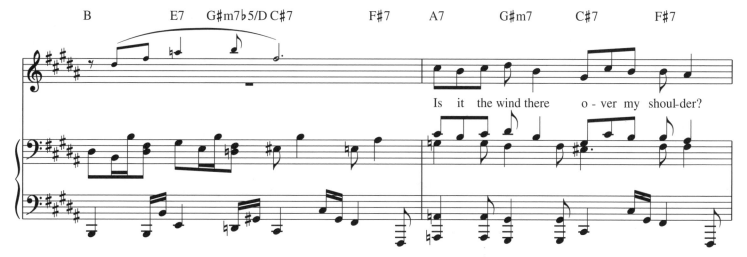

Is it your voice call - ing qui - et - ly? O - ver the hill - top, down in the val - ley,

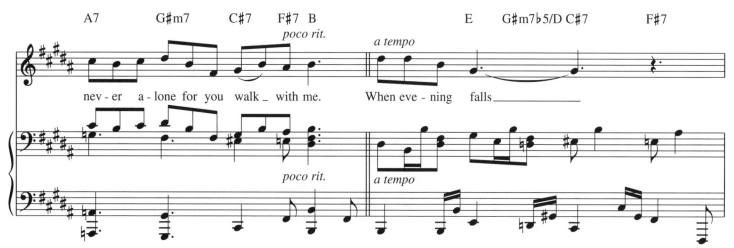

nev - er a - lone for you walk _ with me. When eve - ning falls _____

and the air gets cold-er, _____ when shad-ows cov-er the road I am fol-low-ing

will I be a - lone _____ there in the dark-ness? _____

No, not a - lone, not a-lone and I'll nev-er be... Nev-er a - lone. You are walk-ing, you're walk-ing with

me. Is it the wind there _ o - ver my shoul-der?

*Sing the top line melody in this section for a solo version of the song.

SOMEONE LIKE YOU

from JEKYLL & HYDE

Words by LESLIE BRICUSSE
Music by FRANK WILDHORN

Slowly, with expression

I peered through win-dows, watched life go by.
It's like you took my dreams, made each one real.

Dreamed of to-mor-row,
You reached in-side of me

but stayed in-side.
and made me feel.

The past was hold-ing me,
And now I see a world

THIS IS THE MOMENT
from JEKYLL & HYDE

Words by LESLIE BRICUSSE
Music by FRANK WILDHORN

com-ing___ in-to play, is here and now___ to-day.___ This is the

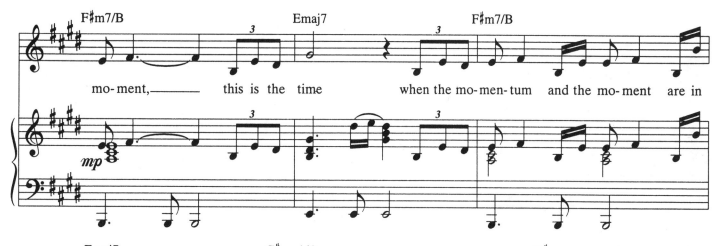

mo-ment,___ this is the time when the mo-men-tum and the mo-ment are in

rhyme. Give me this mo-ment,___ this___ pre-cious chance. I'll

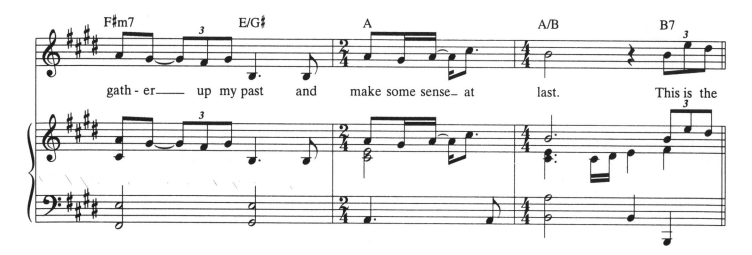

gath-er___ up my past and make some sense_ at last. This is the

mo - ment, when all I've done, all of the
mo - ment, my fi - nal test. Des - ti - ny

dream - ing, schem - ing and scream - ing be - come one! This is the
beck - oned, I nev - er reck - oned sec - ond best. I won't look

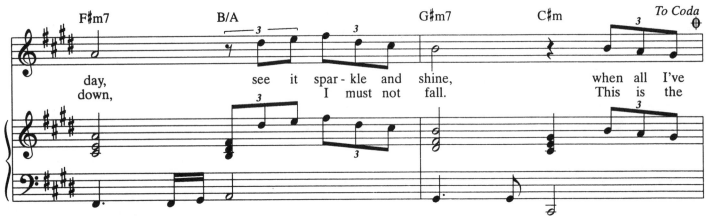

day, see it spar - kle and shine, when all I've
down, I must not fall. This is the

lived for____ be - comes mine! For all these years I've

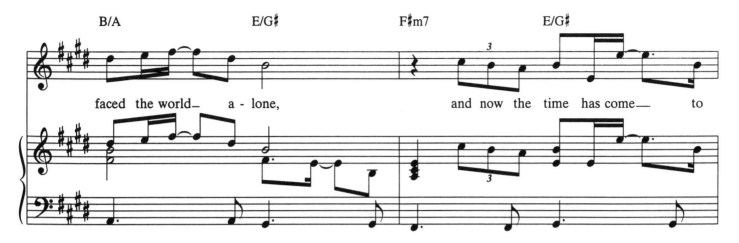

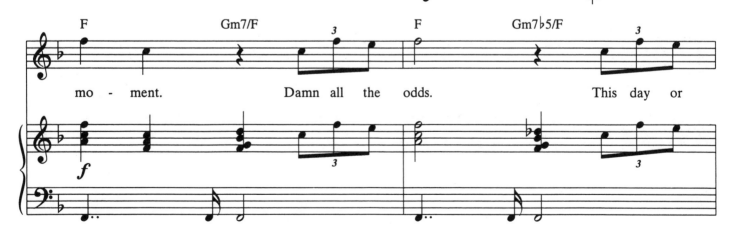

BRING HIM HOME

from LES MISÉRABLES

Music by CLAUDE-MICHEL SCHÖNBERG
Lyrics by HERBERT KRETZMER
and ALAIN BOUBLIL

rest _____ hea - ven blessed. _____ Bring him

poco più mosso   *rall.*

home, _____ bring him home, _____ bring him

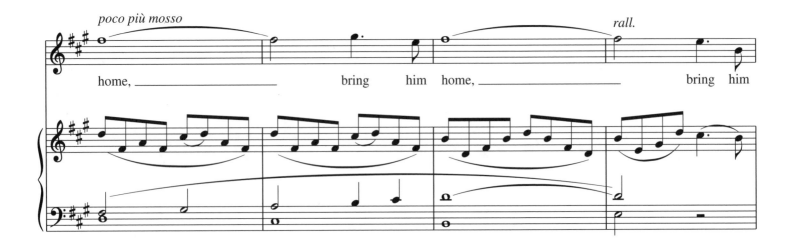

più mosso

home.   He's like the son I might have known   if God had grant-ed me a

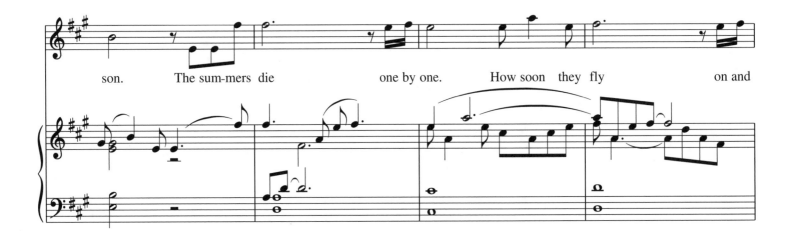

son.   The sum-mers die   one by one.   How soon they fly   on and

on. And I am old and will be gone. Bring him

peace, _____ bring him joy. _____ He is

young, _____ he is on-ly a boy. ____ You can

take, _____ you can give. _____ Let him

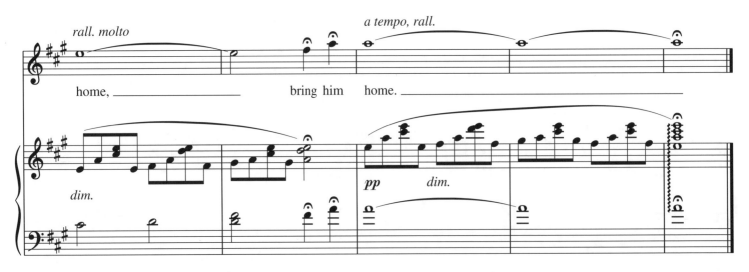

I DREAMED A DREAM

from LES MISÉRABLES

Music by CLAUDE-MICHEL SCHÖNBERG
Lyrics by HERBERT KRETZMER
Original Text by ALAIN BOUBLIL and JEAN-MARC NATEL

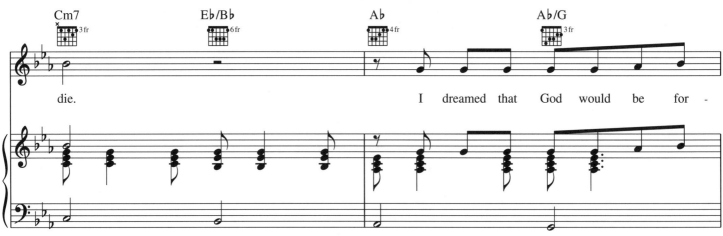

die.

I dreamed that God would be for-

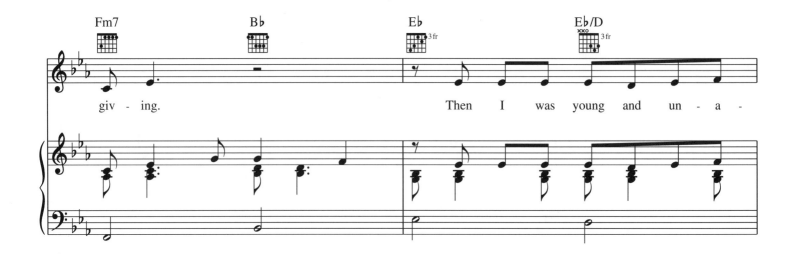

giv - ing.

Then I was young and un - a -

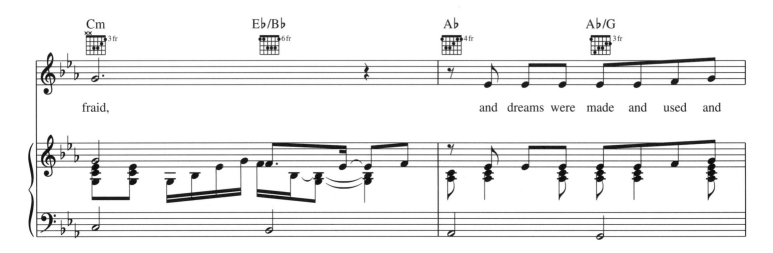

fraid,

and dreams were made and used and

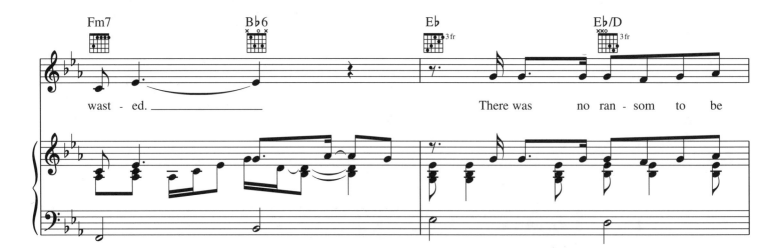

wast - ed. _____

There was no ran - som to be

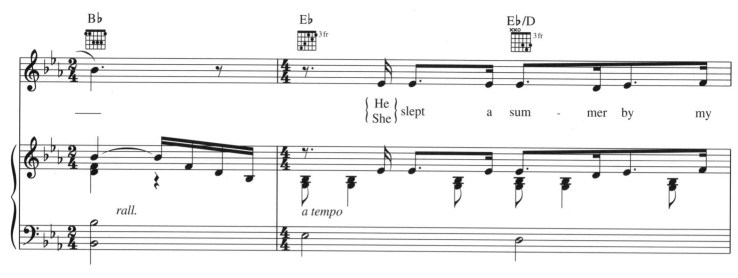

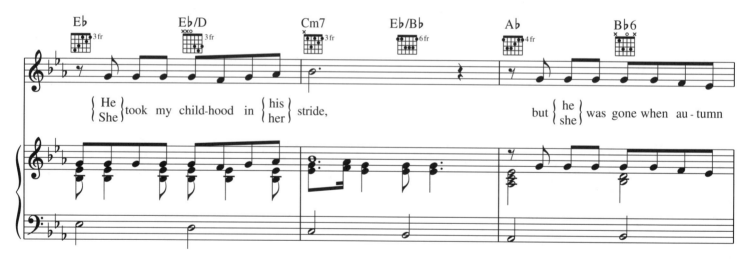

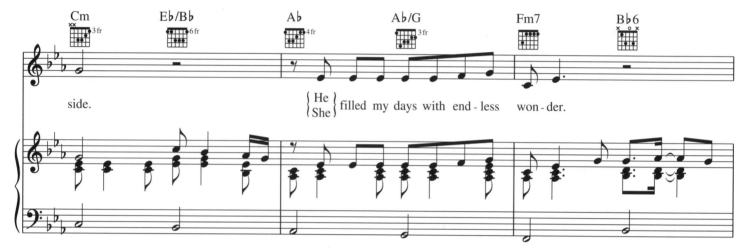

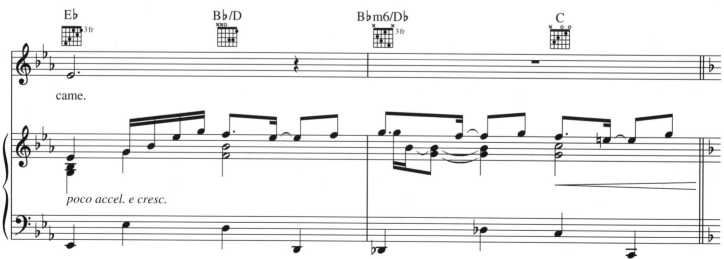

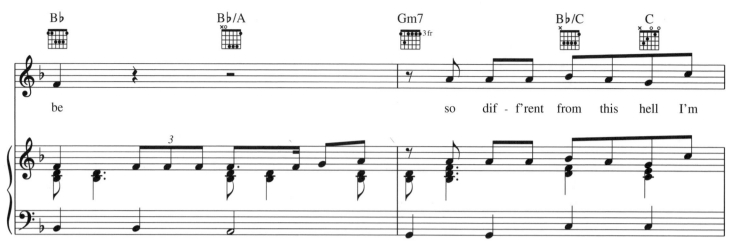

be so dif - f'rent from this hell I'm

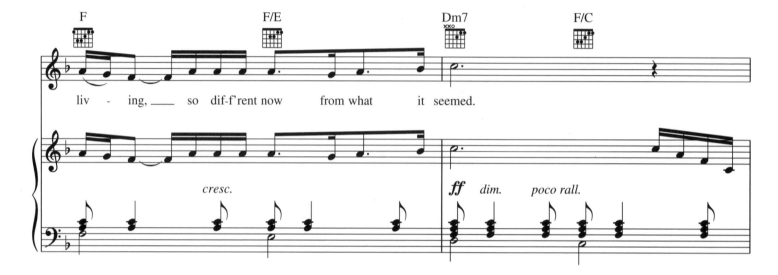

liv - ing, ___ so dif-f'rent now from what it seemed.

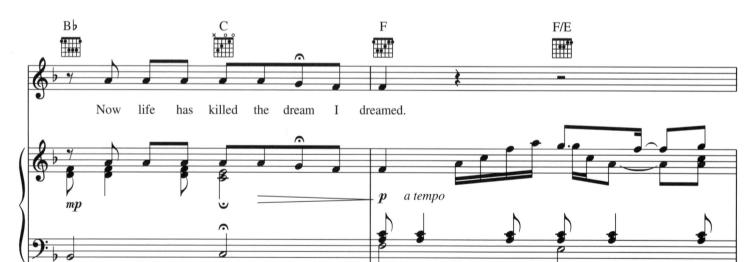

Now life has killed the dream I dreamed.

SHADOWLAND

Disney Presents THE LION KING: THE BROADWAY MUSICAL

Music by LEBO M and HANS ZIMMER
Lyrics by MARK MANCINA and LEBO M

Emotionally, slowly

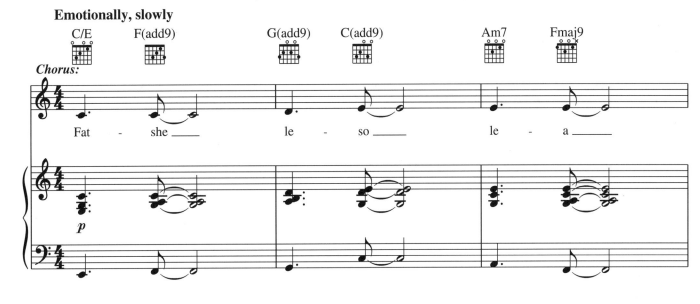

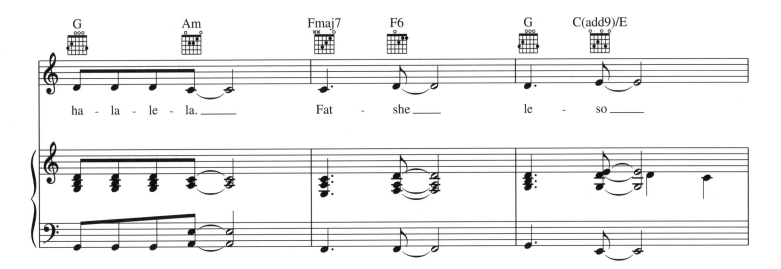

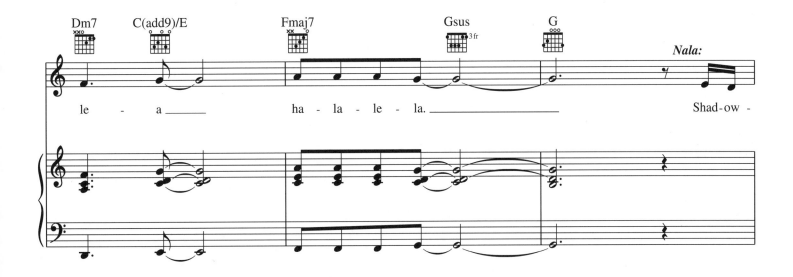

land, _____ the leaves _ have

fall - en. _____ This shad - owed

land, _____ this was our

home.

The ___ riv - er's

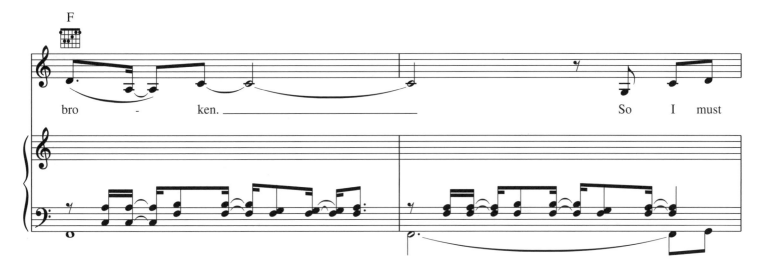

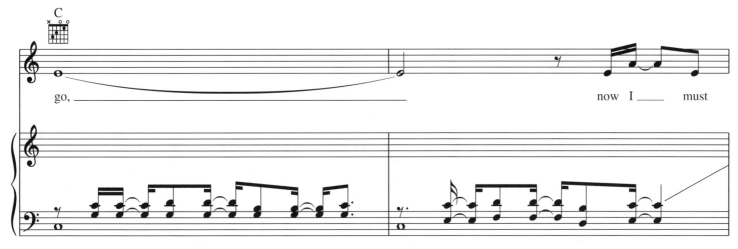

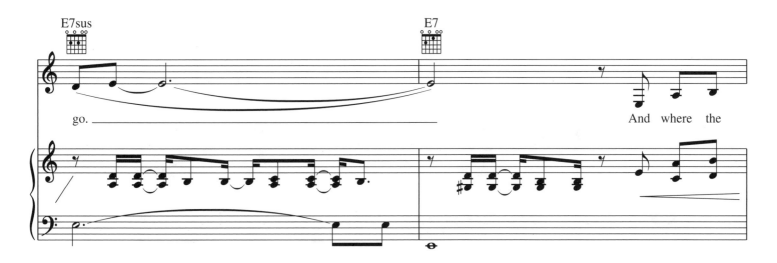

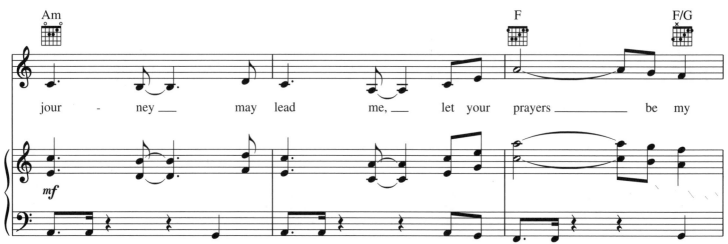

jour - ney __ may lead me, __ let your prayers __ be my

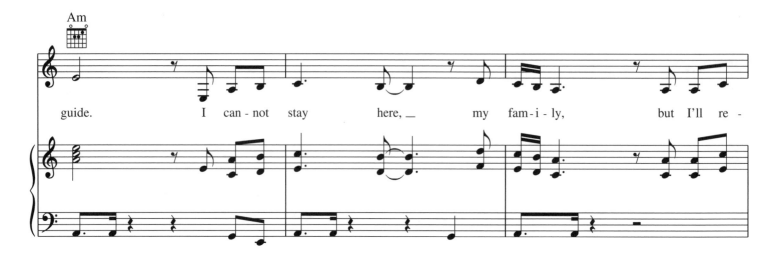

guide. I can-not stay here, __ my fam-i-ly, but I'll re-

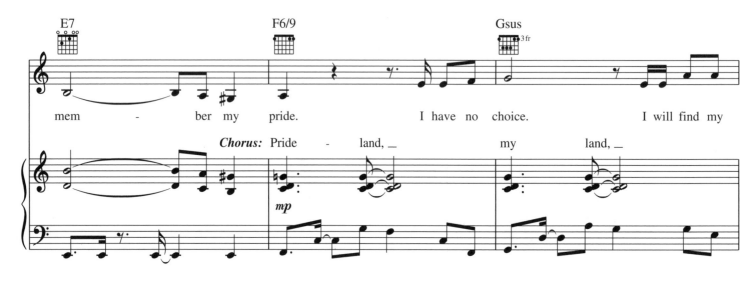

mem - ber my pride. I have no choice. I will find my

Chorus: Pride - land, __ my land, __

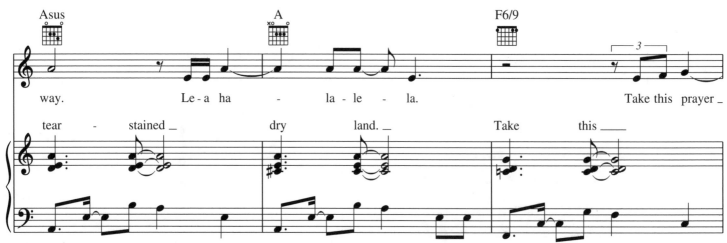

way. Le-a ha - la-le - la. Take this prayer __

tear - stained __ dry land. __ Take this ___

what lies out ___ there. Le-a ha - la-le-la. ___

with you, ___ fat - she ___ le - so. ___

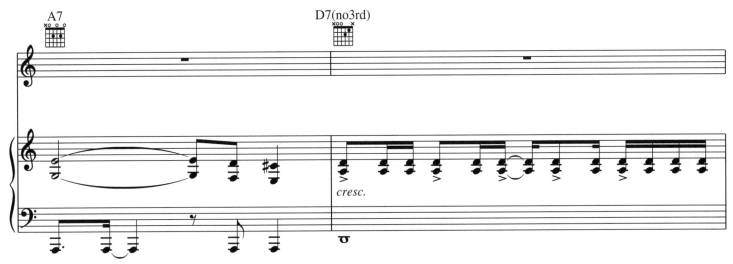

cresc.

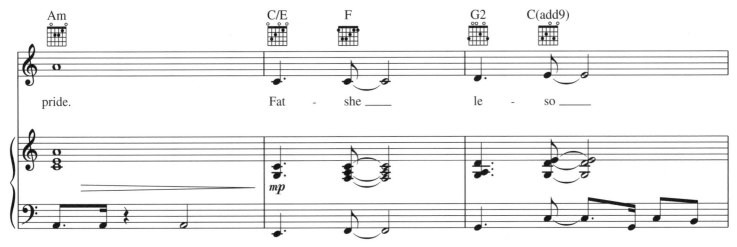

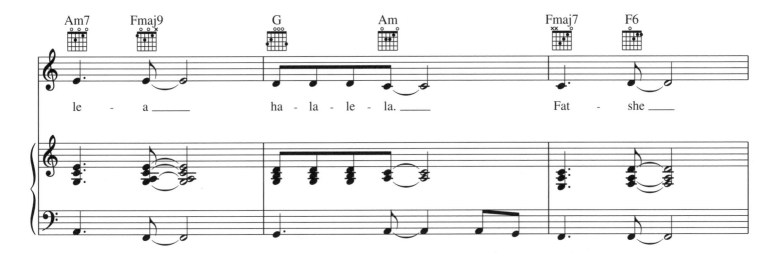

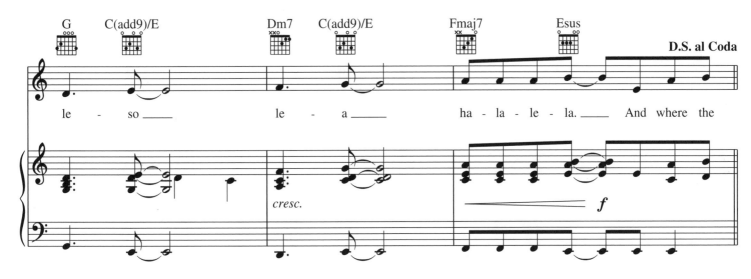

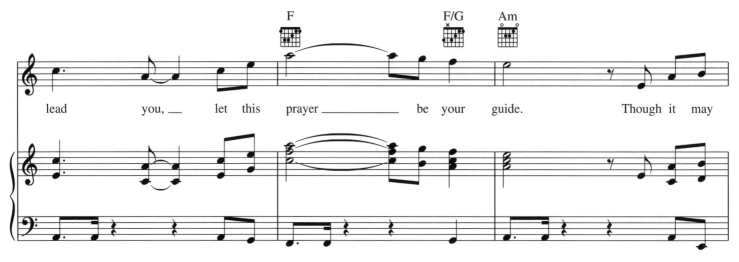

lead you, __ let this prayer _____ be your guide. Though it may

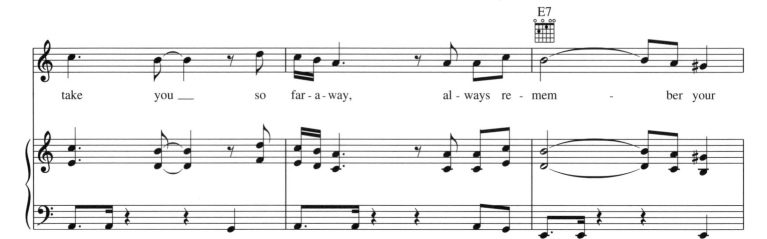

take you __ so far-a-way, al-ways re-mem - ber your

pride. *(ad lib.)* *Nala:* Mm. _____ Gi -

gi-za bu-ya-bo. ____ Be-si-bo, ____ my peo-ple, be-si-bo. ____

THEY LIVE IN YOU
Disney Presents THE LION KING: THE BROADWAY MUSICAL

Music and Lyrics by MARK MANCINA,
JAY RIFKIN and LEBO M

Spiritually, steadily

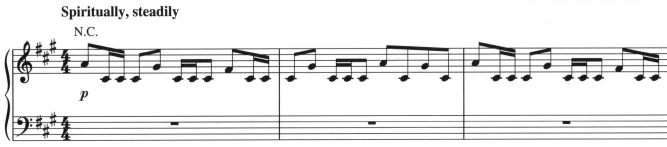

In - gon-ya - ma nengw' en - a - ma-ba - la.

In - gon-ya - ma nengw' en - a - ma-ba - la. Night

and the spir - it __ of life call - ing.

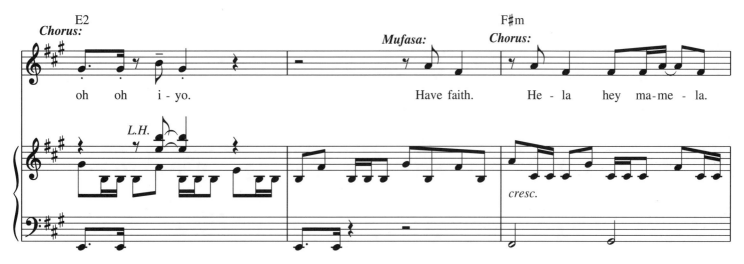

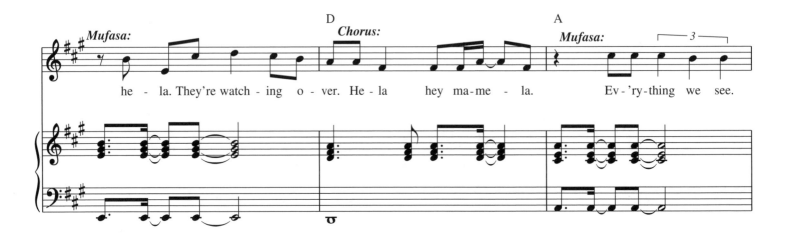

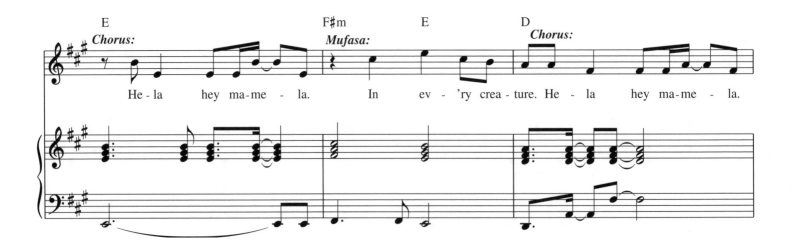

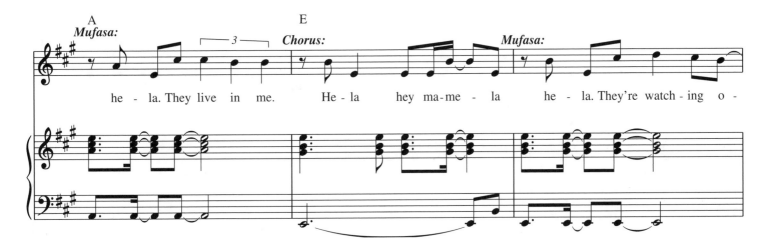

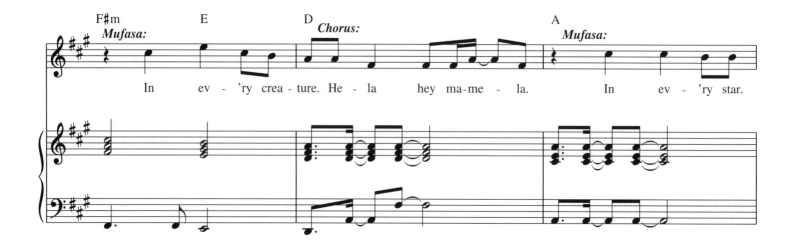

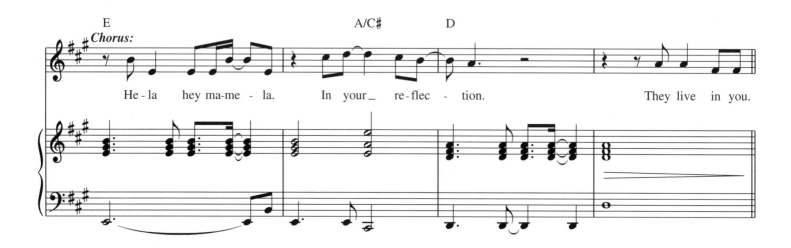

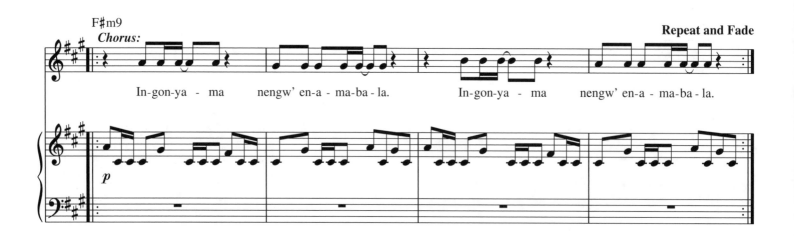

ALL I ASK OF YOU
from THE PHANTOM OF THE OPERA

Music by ANDREW LLOYD WEBBER
Lyrics by CHARLES HART
Additional Lyrics by RICHARD STILGOE

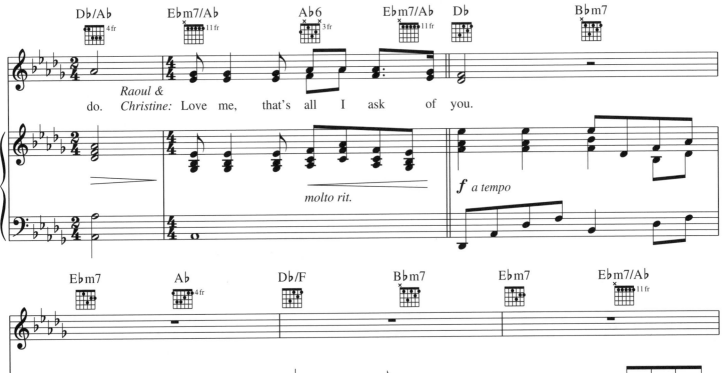

Raoul &
do. Christine: Love me, that's all I ask of you.

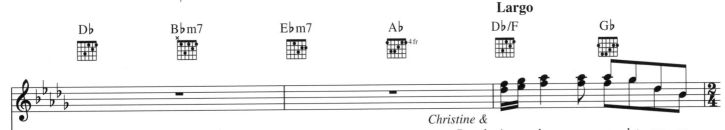

Largo

Christine &
Raoul: An-y-where you go, let me go

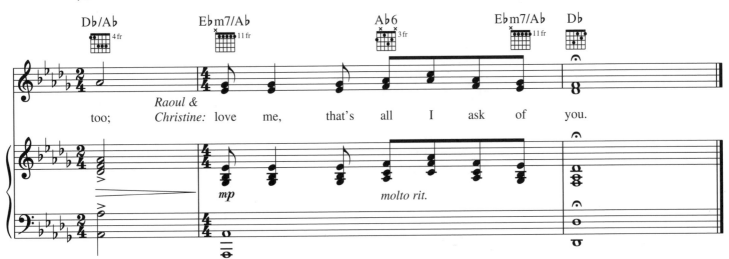

Raoul &
too; Christine: love me, that's all I ask of you.

THE MUSIC OF THE NIGHT
from THE PHANTOM OF THE OPERA

Music by ANDREW LLOYD WEBBER
Lyrics by CHARLES HART
Additional Lyrics by RICHARD STILGOE

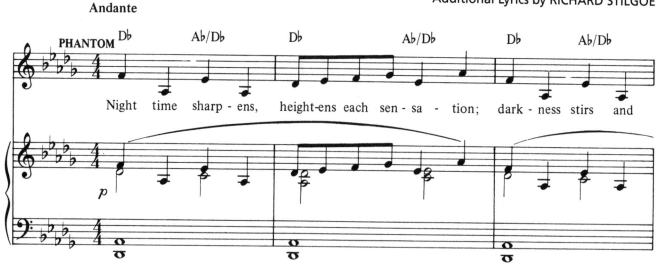

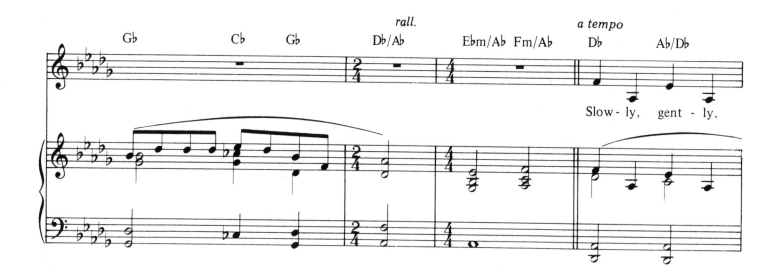

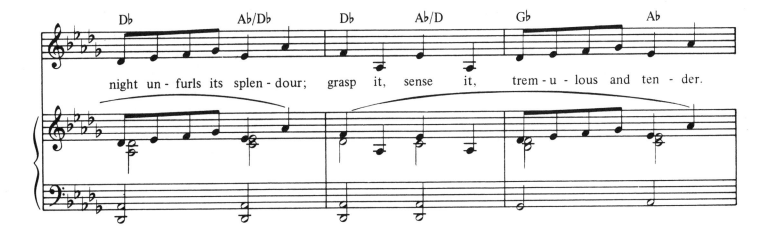

night un - furls its splen - dour; grasp it, sense it, trem - u - lous and ten - der.

Turn your face a - way from the gar-ish light of day, turn your thoughts a-way from cold, un - feel-ing

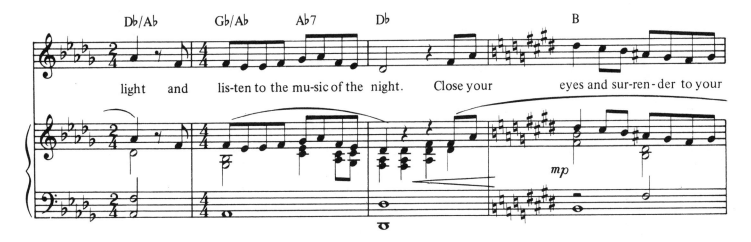

light and lis-ten to the mu-sic of the night. Close your eyes and sur-ren - der to your

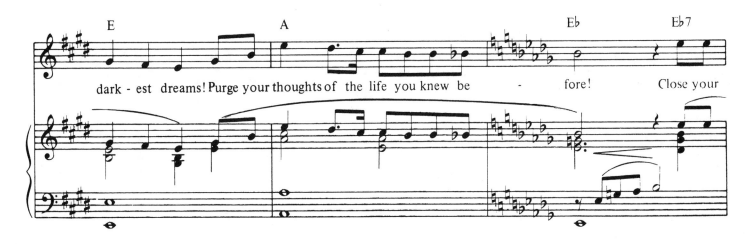

dark - est dreams! Purge your thoughts of the life you knew be - fore! Close your

eyes let your spi-rit start to soar and you'll live as you've nev-er lived be - fore.

Soft - ly, deft - ly, mu-sic shall ca-ress you. Hear it, feel it,

se -cret-ly po-ssess you. O -pen up your mind. let your fan - ta - sies un-wind in this

dark-ness which you know you can-not fight, the dark-ness of the mu-sic of the

WHEN YOU GOT IT, FLAUNT IT

from THE PRODUCERS

Words and Music by
MEL BROOKS

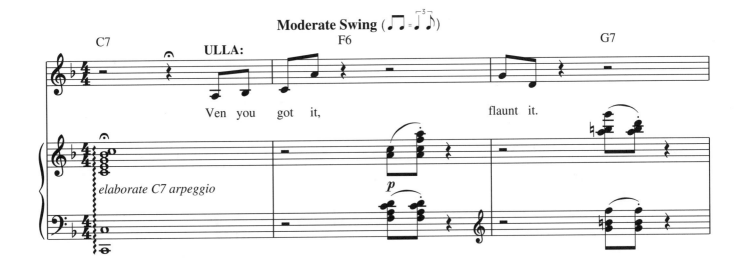

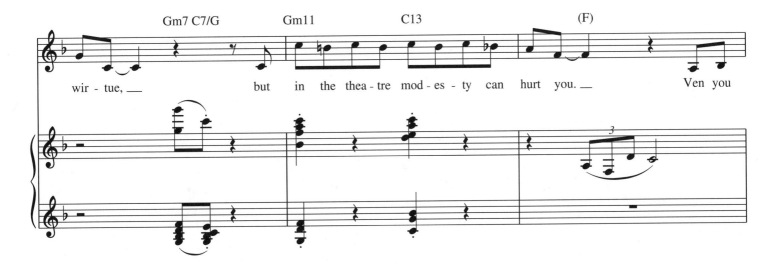

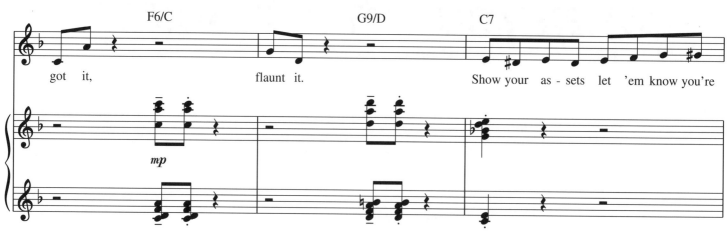

got it, flaunt it. Show your as - sets let 'em know you're

proud. Your good - ies you must push, stick your chest out, shake your tush, ven you

got it, shout _ it out loud! _ Ven you got it

Cool Swing

show it put your hid - den trea - sures on dis - play

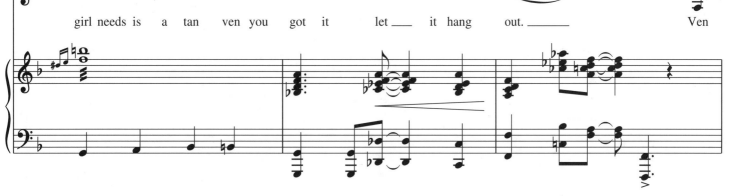

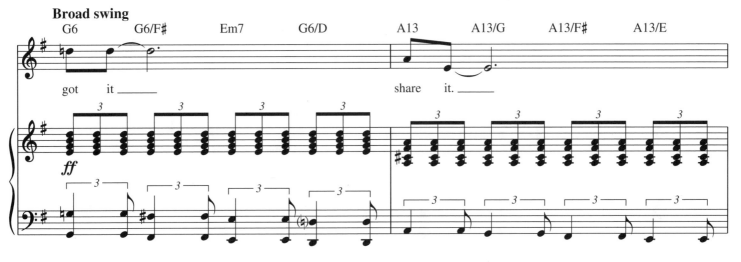

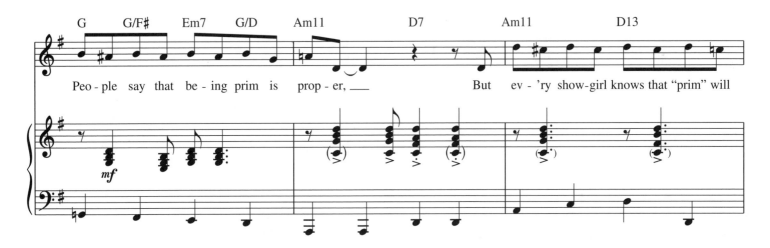

give it. _____ Don't be self - ish, give it all a -

vay! _____ Don't be

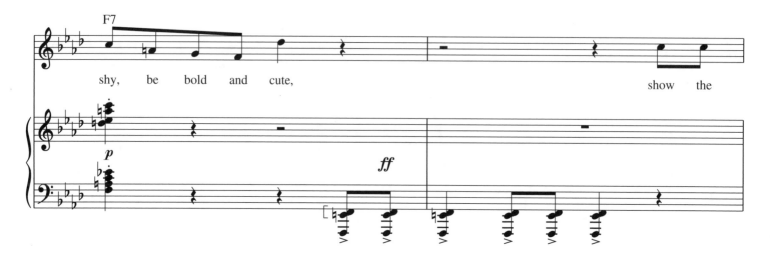

shy, be bold and cute, show the

boys that birth - day suit ven you

"Going home"

Samba-straight 8ths

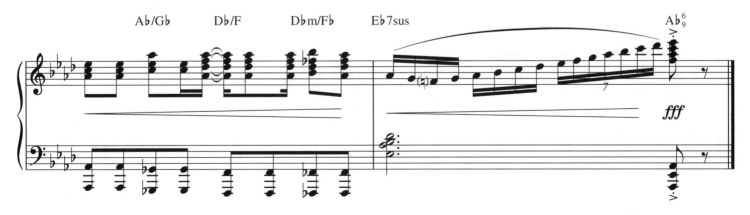

'TIL HIM
from THE PRODUCERS

Words and Music by
MEL BROOKS

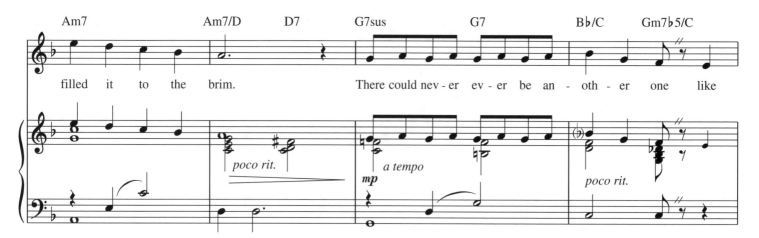

filled it to the brim. There could nev-er ev-er be an-oth-er one like

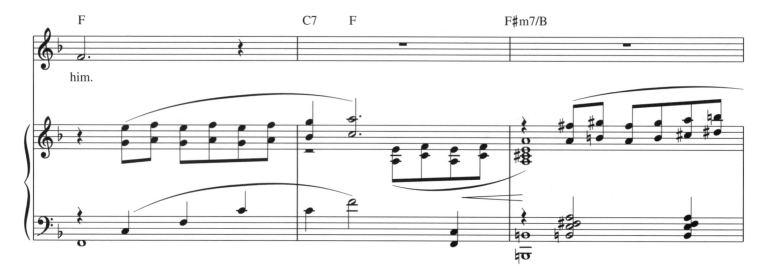

him.

MAX:
No one ev-er ev-er real-ly knew me 'til

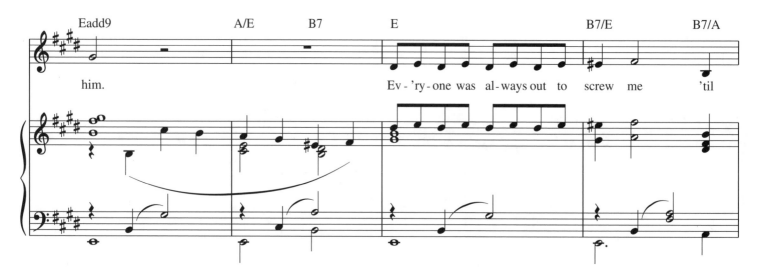

him.
Ev-'ry-one was al-ways out to screw me 'til

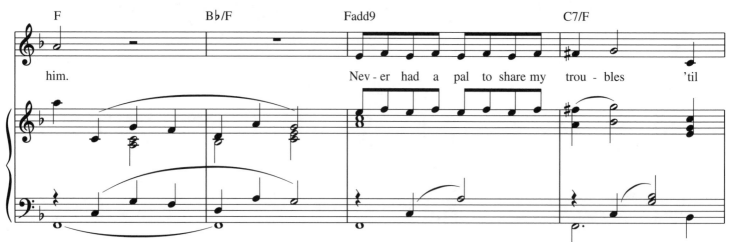

him.   Nev - er had a pal to share my trou - bles   'til

LEO & MAX:

him.   He   filled up   my   emp - ty life

LEO:

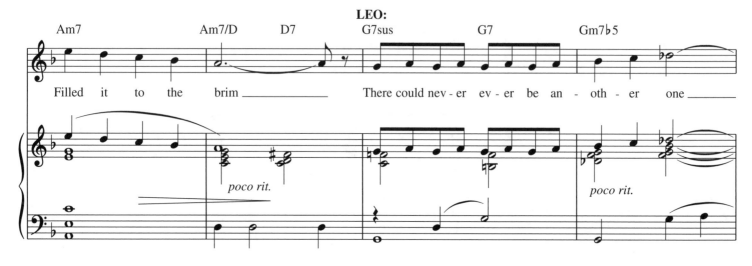

Filled it   to   the   brim _____ There could nev - er ev - er be an - oth - er   one ____

Slowly

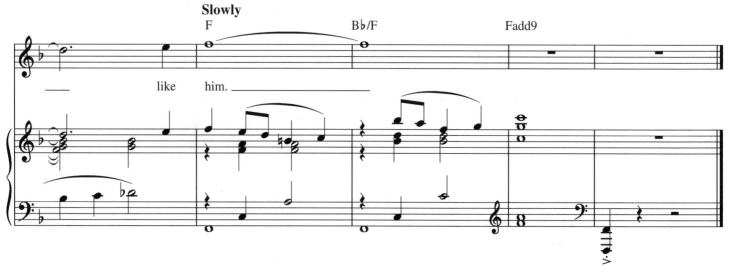

____   like   him. _____

I WILL NEVER LEAVE YOU

from SIDE SHOW

Words by BILL RUSSELL
Music by HENRY KRIEGER

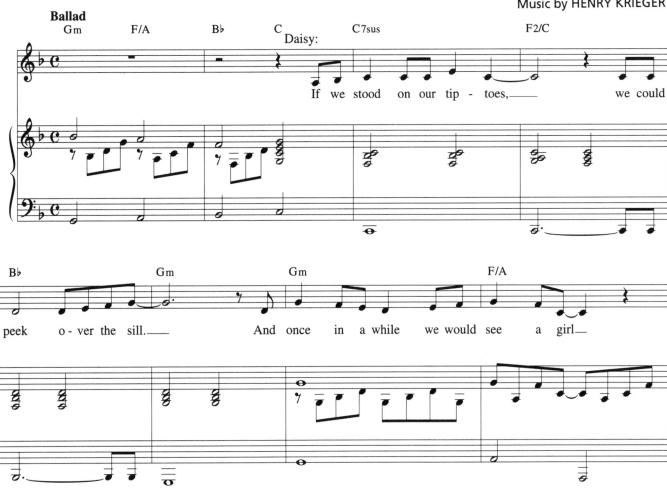

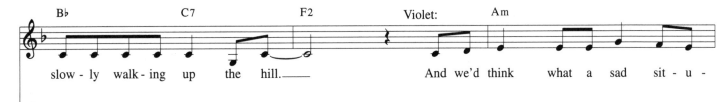

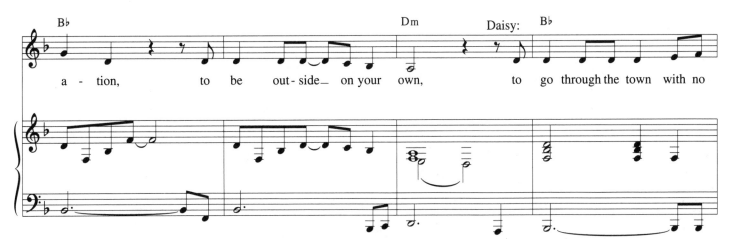

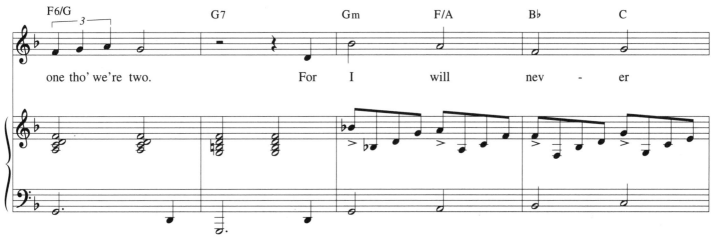

one tho' we're two. For I will nev - er

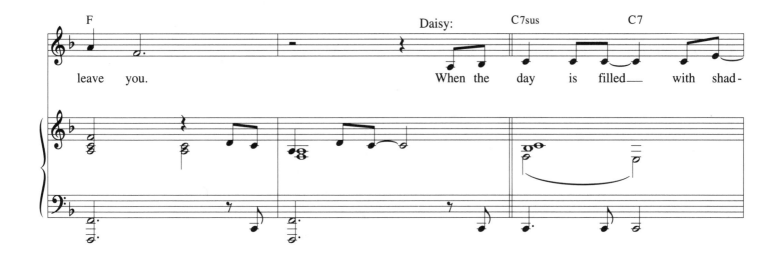

leave you. When the day is filled___ with shad -

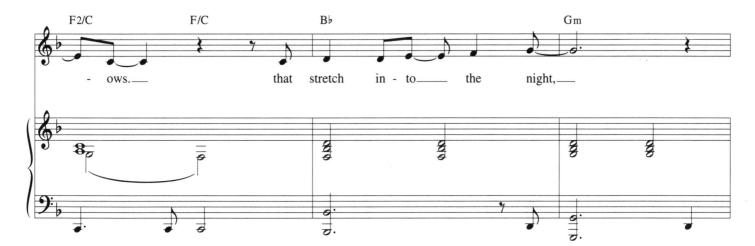

- ows.___ that stretch in - to___ the night,___

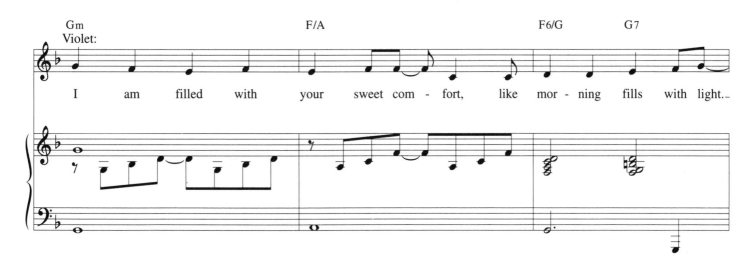

I am filled with your sweet com - fort, like mor - ning fills with light.___

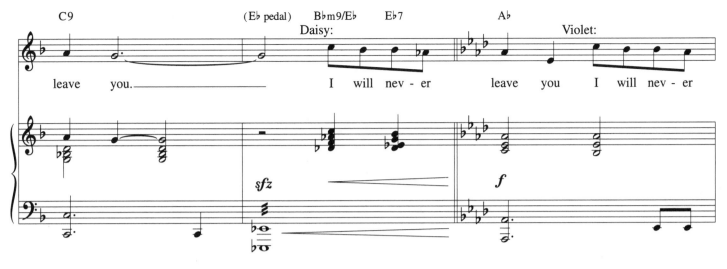

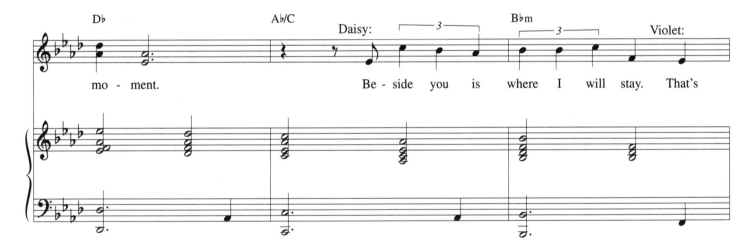

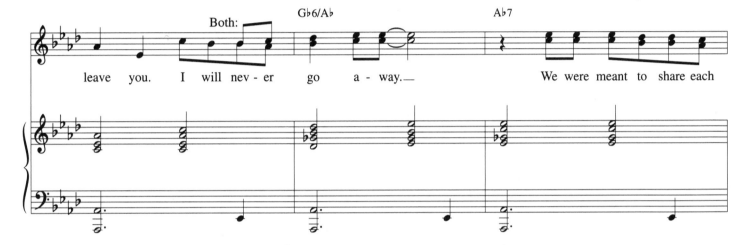

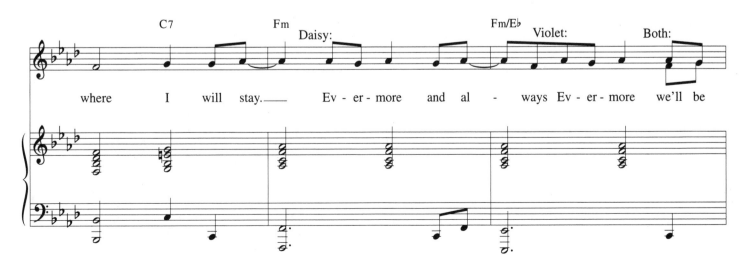

one tho' we're two. One tho' we're two. For I will

nev - er I will nev - er

I will nev - er leave you

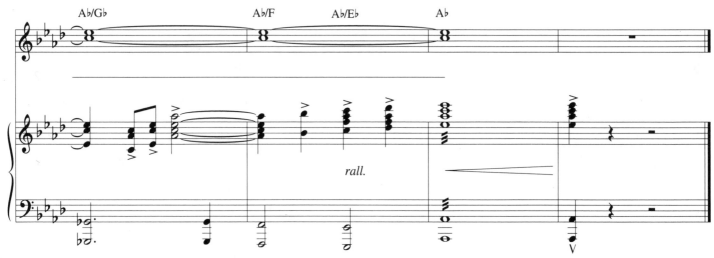

WHO WILL LOVE ME AS I AM?

from SIDE SHOW

Words by BILL RUSSELL
Music by HENRY KRIEGER

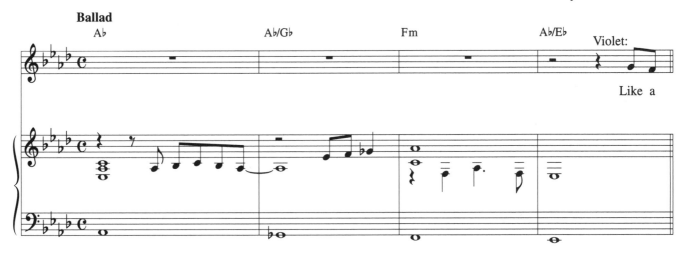

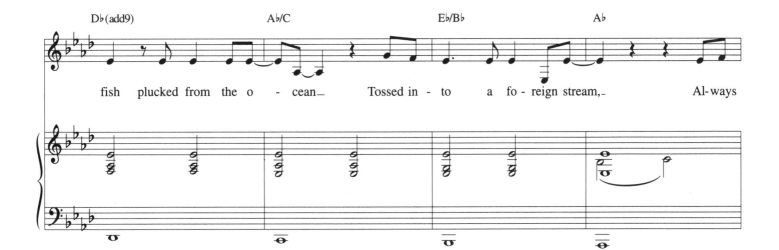

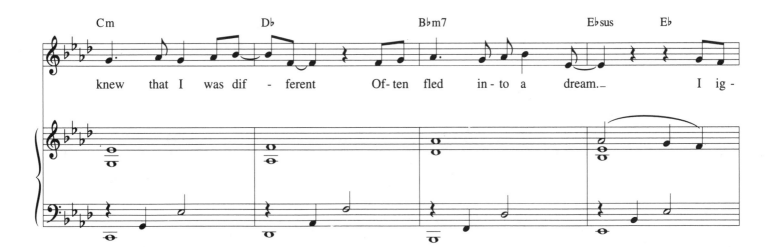

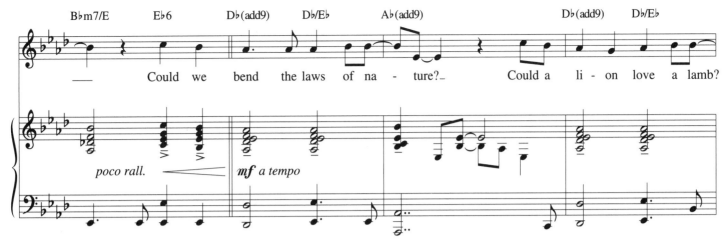

Could we bend the laws of na - ture?_ Could a li - on love a lamb?

poco rall.   _mf a tempo_

Who could see be - yond this sur - face? Who will love me as I am?_

Both:

Who will e - ver call to say "I love_ you"? Send me

poco rall.   _mf_

flow - ers or a tel - e - gram?_ Who could proud - ly stand_ be - side_

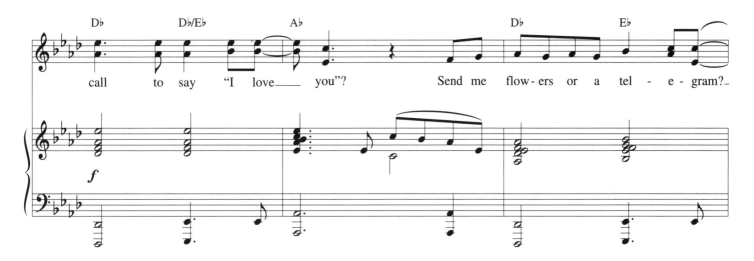

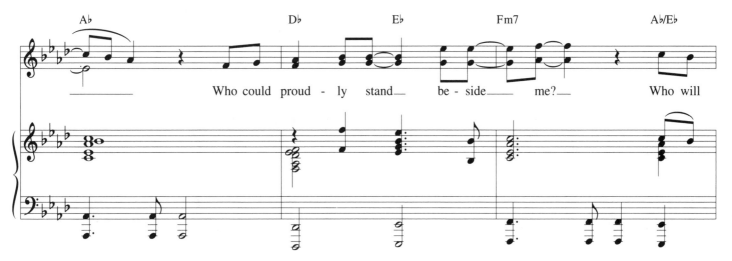

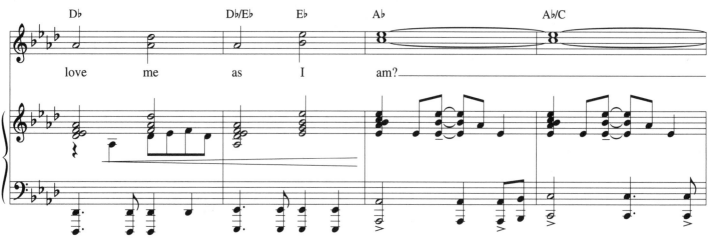

love me as I am?

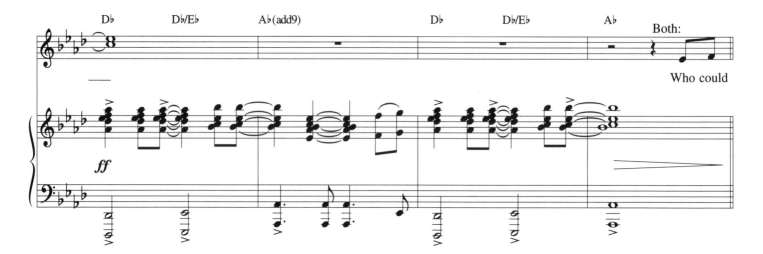

Who could

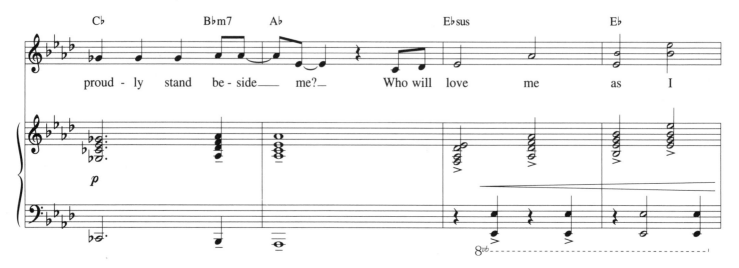

proud-ly stand be-side___ me?___ Who will love me as I

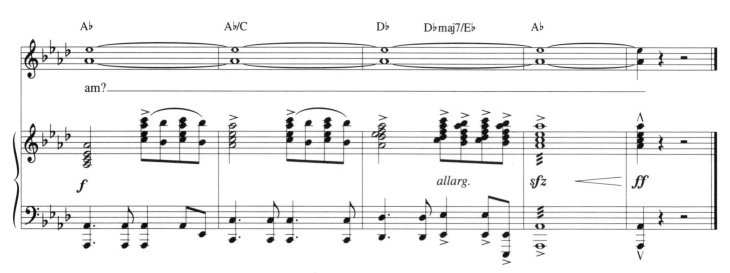

am?___

MY CHILD WILL FORGIVE ME

from PARADE

Music and Lyrics by
JASON ROBERT BROWN

Valse lente

My child will for-give me for

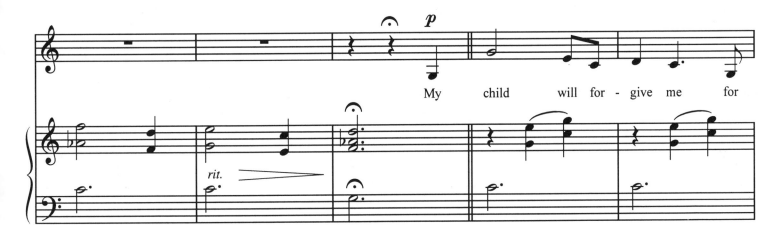

rais - in' her poor, and for tak - in' her out of the school.

My child will for-give me for not do - in' more to pro-

tect her from men who are____ cruel. And my child will for-

poco rit. *a tempo*

give me for clos - in' my eyes to the dan - gers of grow-in'____ too

fast. My____ child will for - give me with tears in her

pp

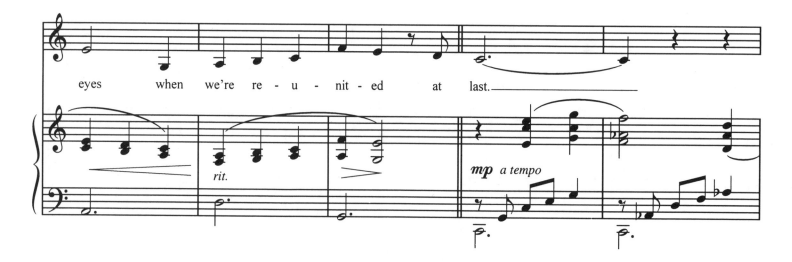

eyes when we're re - u - nit - ed at last._____

rit. *mp a tempo*

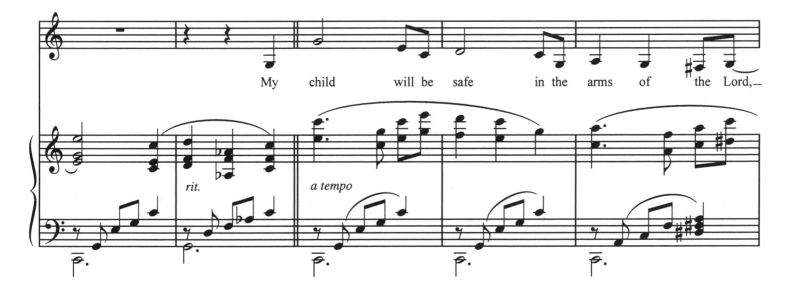

My child will be safe in the arms of the Lord,—

rit. *a tempo*

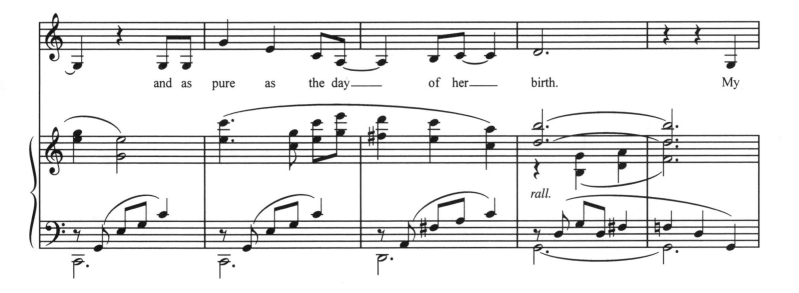

and as pure as the day_____ of her_____ birth. My

rall.

child will be co - zied and blessed and a - dored as she

a tempo

YOU DON'T KNOW THIS MAN
from PARADE

Music and Lyrics by
JASON ROBERT BROWN

Poco rubato throughout (♩ = 116)

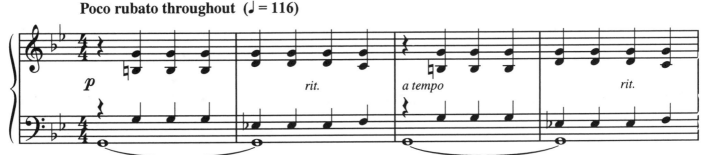

You don't know this man. You don't know a thing.

You come here with these hor-ri-fy-ing sto-ries, these con-temp-ti-ble con-ceits, and you

say you un-der-stand how a man's heart beats. And you don't know a thing.

You don't know this man.

poco animato   *rit.*   ***p*** *a tempo*

You don't e - ven try.   When a man writes his

poco accel. e cresc.

moth-er ev-'ry Sun-day, pays his bills be-fore they're due, works so hard to feed his fam-'ly, there's your

poco accel. e cresc.

mur-der-er for you! And you stand here spit-ting words that you know aren't true. Then

allarg.

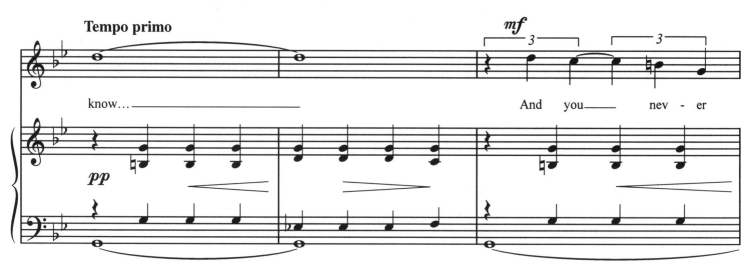

Tempo primo

know... And you never

will. Not from me, not from an-y-one who knows him, not a

mor-sel, not a crumb, not a clue. I have

Freely

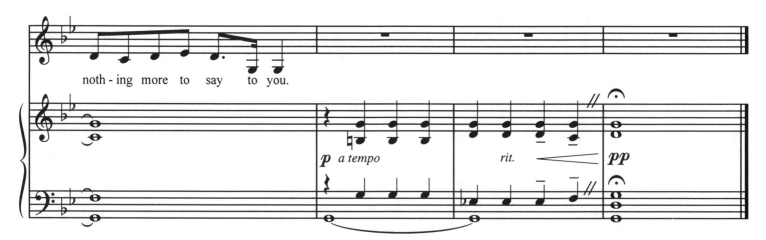

noth-ing more to say to you.

ONE SONG GLORY

from RENT

Words and Music by
JONATHAN LARSON

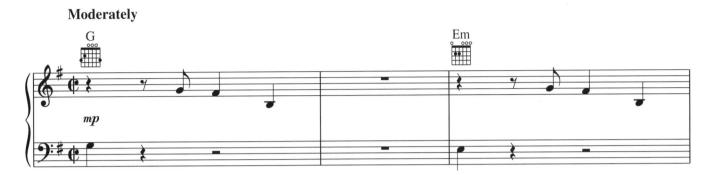

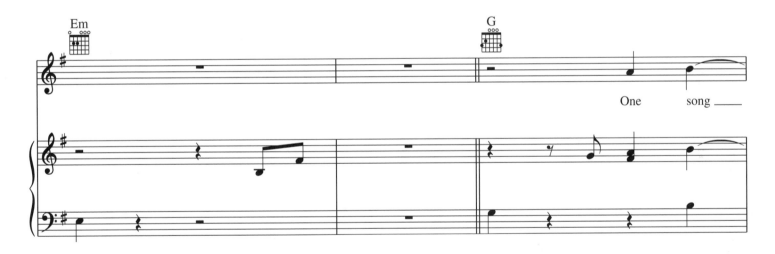

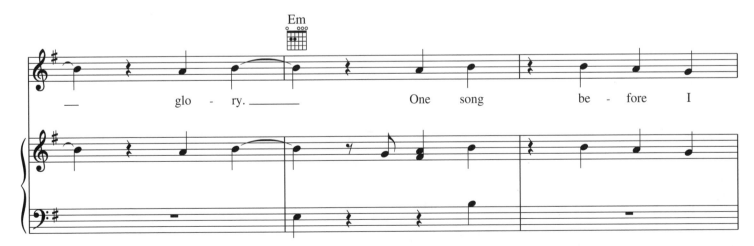

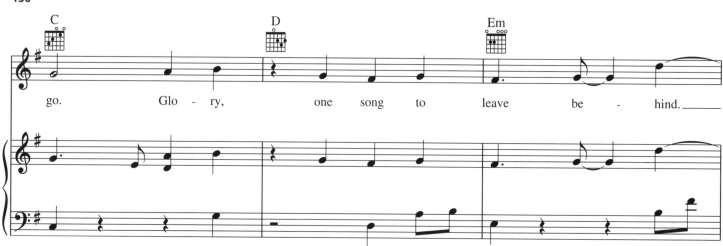

go. Glo-ry, one song to leave be - hind.____

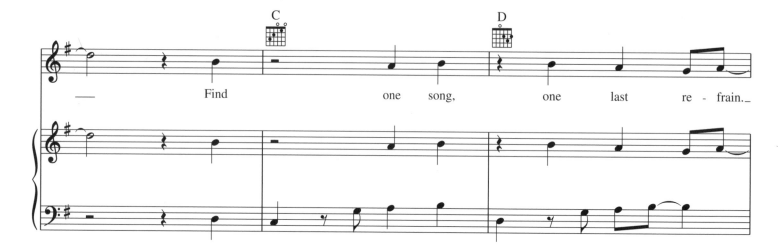

____ Find one song, one last re - frain.__

____ Glo - ry ____ from the pret -ty boy front man ____

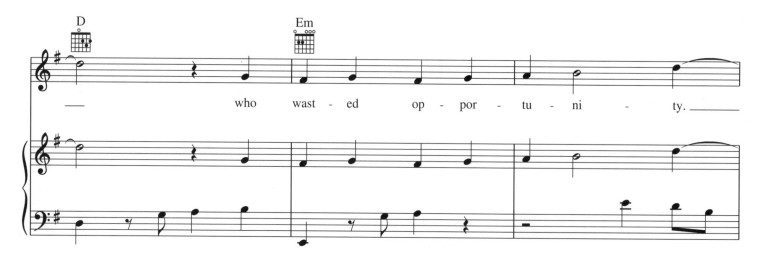

____ who wast - ed op - por - tu - ni - ty. ____

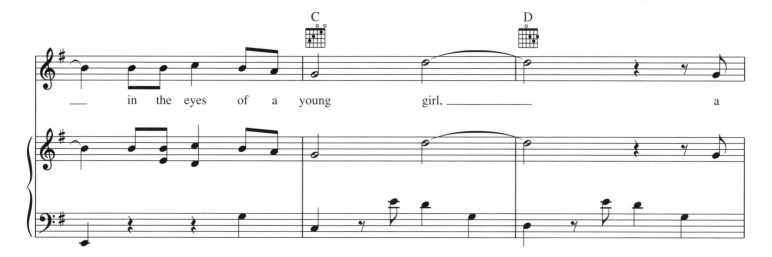

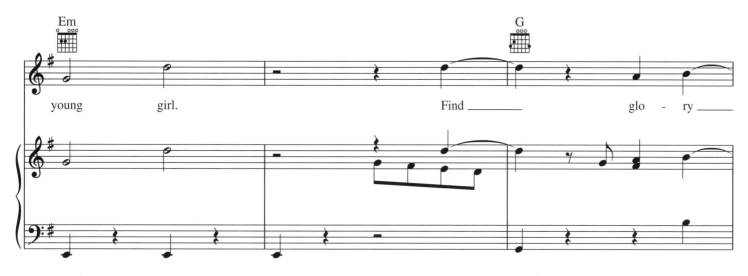

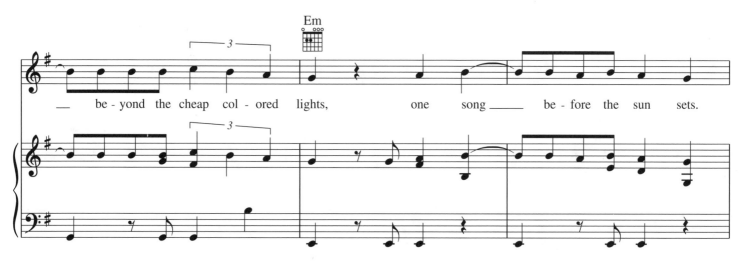

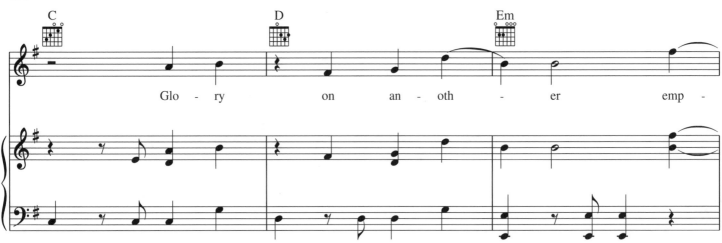

Glo - ry on an - oth - er emp -

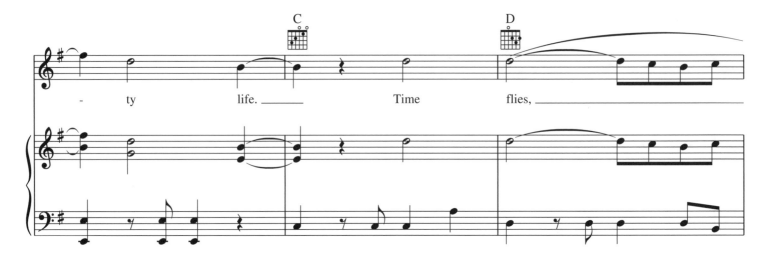

- ty life. _____ Time flies, _____

_____ time dies. _____

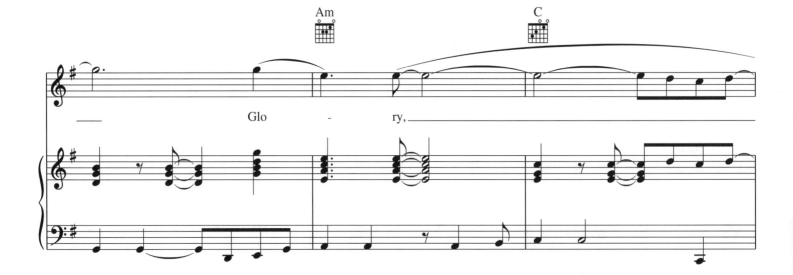

_____ Glo - ry, _____

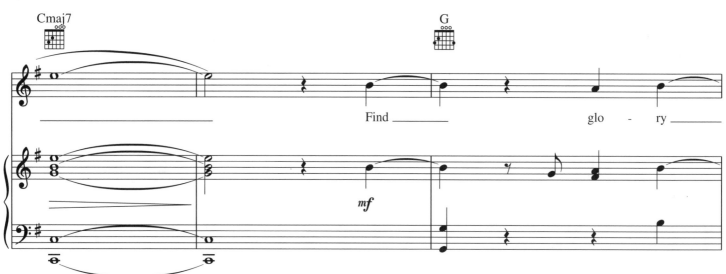

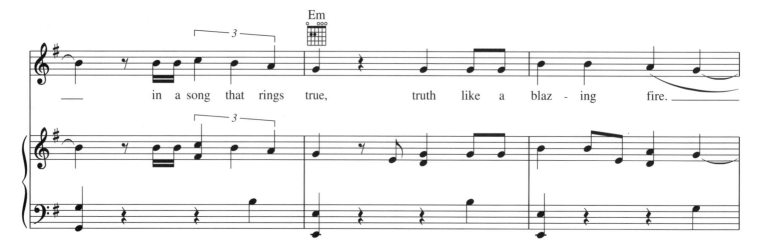

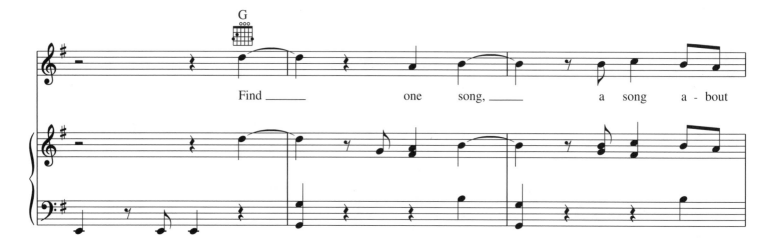

love. Glo - ry _____ from the soul of a young man, _____

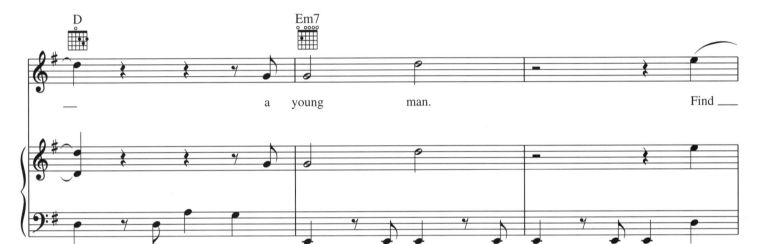

_____ a young man. Find _____

_____ the one song be - fore the vi - rus takes hold, glo - ry

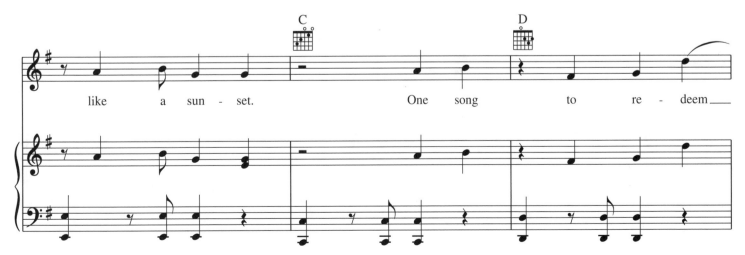

like a sun - set. One song to re - deem _____

SEASONS OF LOVE

from RENT

Words and Music by
JONATHAN LARSON

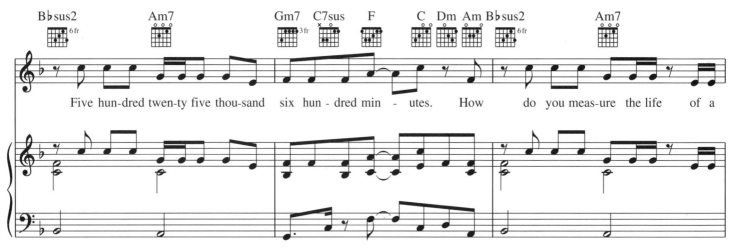

Five hun-dred twen-ty five thou-sand six hun-dred min - utes. How do you meas-ure the life of a

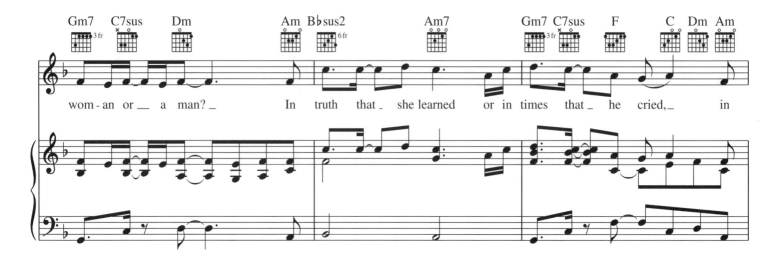

wom-an or __ a man? __ In truth that __ she learned or in times that __ he cried, __ in

bridg - es __ he burned or the way that she died. _____ It's time now to sing out, though the

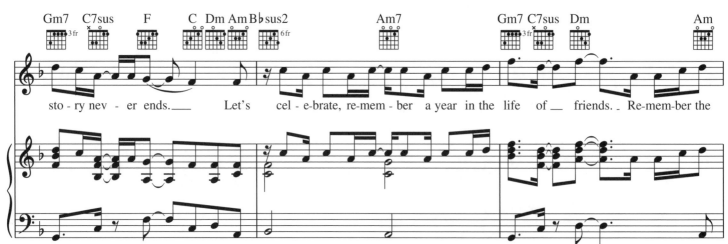

sto-ry nev - er ends. ___ Let's cel-e-brate, re-mem - ber a year in the life of __ friends. _ Re-mem-ber the

MORE THAN A WOMAN

from the Broadway Musical SATURDAY NIGHT FEVER

Words and Music by BARRY GIBB,
MAURICE GIBB and ROBIN GIBB

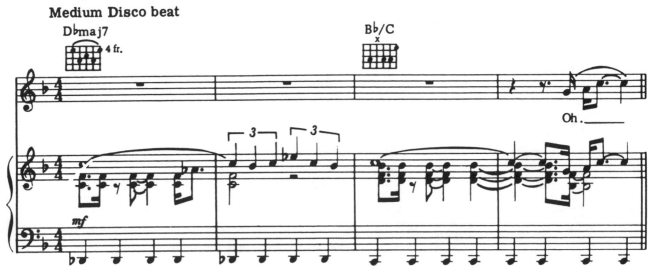

Girl, I've known you ver - y well. I've seen you grow-in' ev - 'ry day.__ I nev-
There are sto-ries old__ and true of peo-ple so__ in love__ like you__ and me,__

er real - ly looked__ be-fore,__ but now you take my breath a - way.__
and I__ can see__ my-self__ let his - to - ry re-peat it - self.__ Re-

Sud - den - ly___ you're in___ my life,___ part of ev - 'ry - thing___ I do. You
flect - ing how___ I feel for you,___ think - in' 'bout___ those peo - ple then, I

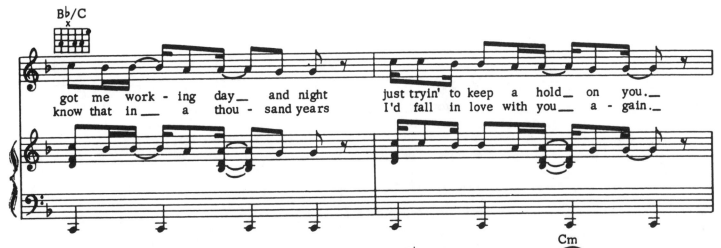

got me work - ing day___ and night just tryin' to keep a hold___ on you.___
know that in___ a thou - sand years I'd fall in love with you___ a - gain.___

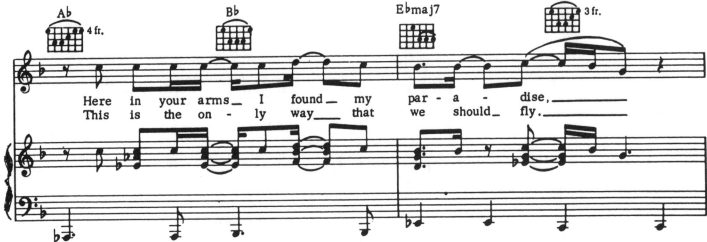

Here in your arms___ I found___ my par - a - dise,_____
This is the on - ly way___ that we should___ fly._____

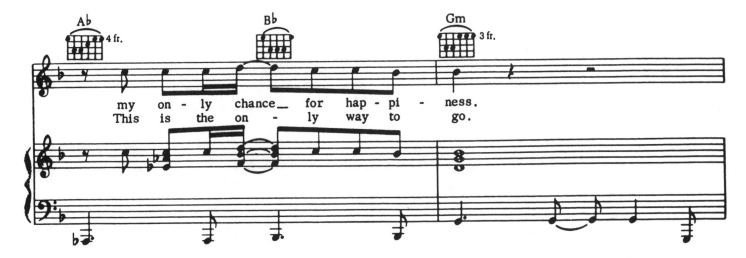

my on - ly chance___ for hap - pi - ness.
This is the on - ly way to go.

150

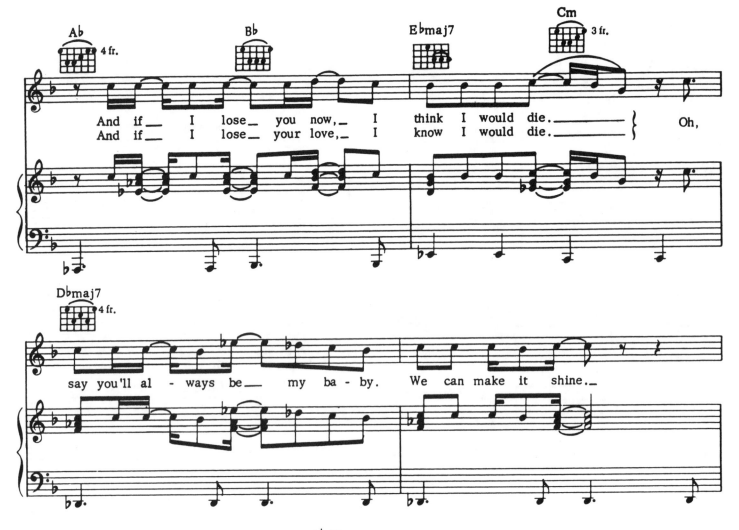

STAYIN' ALIVE
from the Broadway Musical SATURDAY NIGHT FEVER

Words and Music by BARRY GIBB,
MAURICE GIBB and ROBIN GIBB

Medium Rock beat

Well, you can tell

— by the way I use— my walk,— I'm a wom-an's man: no time to talk.—
— get— low and I— get high,— and if I— can't get ei-ther, I real-ly try. Got the

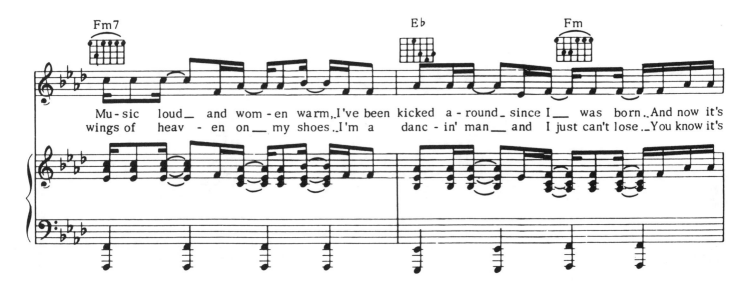

Mu-sic loud— and wom-en warm, I've been kicked a-round— since I— was born. And now it's
wings of heav-en on— my shoes. I'm a danc-in' man— and I just can't lose. You know it's

all right.__ It's O K.__ And you may look_ the oth - er way.__
all right.__ It's O K.__ I'll live to see__ an-oth - er day.__

We can try__ to un-der - stand__ the New York Times' ef - fect__ on man.__

Wheth-er you're a broth-er or wheth-er you're a moth-er, you're stay - in' a - live,__ stay-in' a-live.__

Feel the cit-y break-in' and ev - 'ry-bod-y shak-in', and we're stay-in' a - live,__ stay-in' a-live.__

Some-bod-y help me.____ Some-bod-y help_ me, yeah.____

Fm7

Bb7

____ Life go-in' no-where.____

Fm7

Some-bod-y help_ me, yeah.____ I'm stay-in' a-live._

THEY SAY IT'S WONDERFUL
from the Stage Production ANNIE GET YOUR GUN

Words and Music by
IRVING BERLIN

THERE'S NO BUSINESS LIKE SHOW BUSINESS

from the Stage Production ANNIE GET YOUR GUN

Words and Music by
IRVING BERLIN

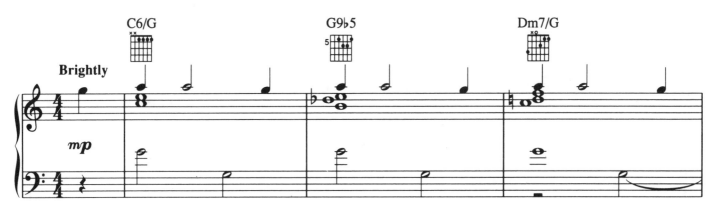

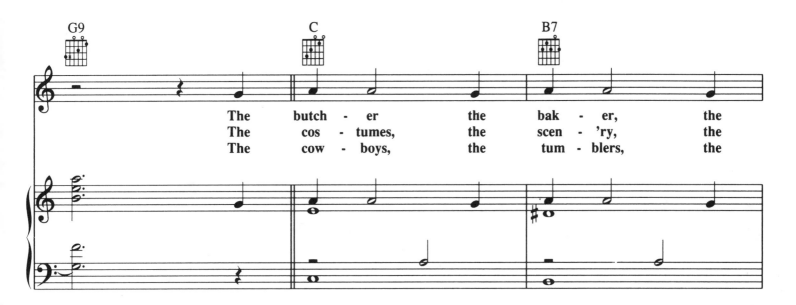

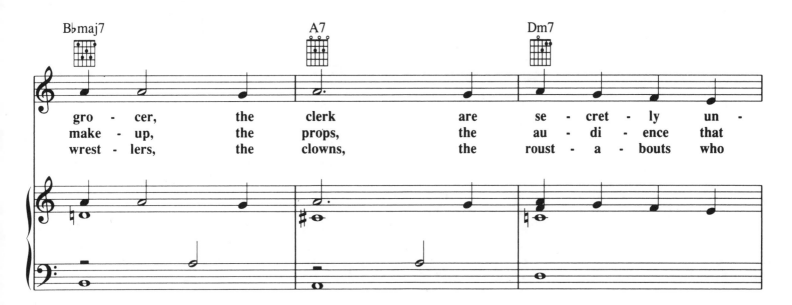

MAYBE THIS TIME
from the Musical CABARET

Words by FRED EBB
Music by JOHN KANDER

MEIN HERR
from the Musical CABARET

Words by FRED EBB
Music by JOHN KANDER

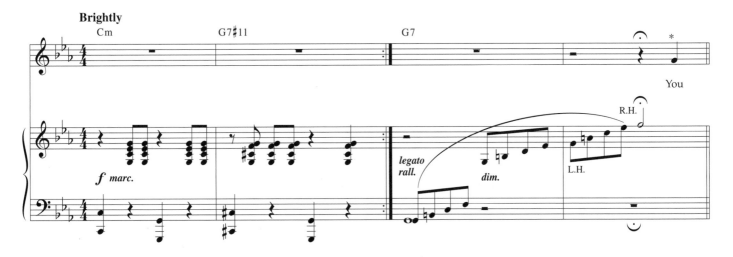

have to un-der-stand the way I am, mein Herr. A ti-ger is a ti-ger, not a
con-ti-nent of Eu-rope is so wide, mein Herr. Not on-ly up and down, but side to

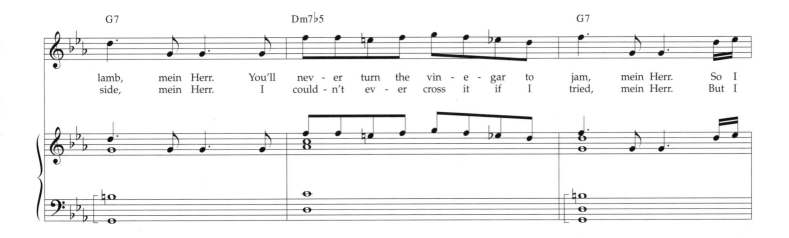

lamb, mein Herr. You'll nev-er turn the vin-e-gar to jam, mein Herr. So I
side, mein Herr. I could-n't ev-er cross it if I tried, mein Herr. But I

Melody is written an octave higher than sung.

do what I do. When I'm through then I'm through and I'm through. Too-dle oo! Bye bye mein
do what I can, inch by inch, step by step, mile by mile, man by man.

Slowly at first, then gradually faster

lie - ber Herr,_____ Fare - well mein lie - ber Herr._____
eye, mein Herr,_____ or won - der why, mein Herr._____

_____ It was a fine af - fair_____ but now it's
_____ I've al - ways said that I_____ was a

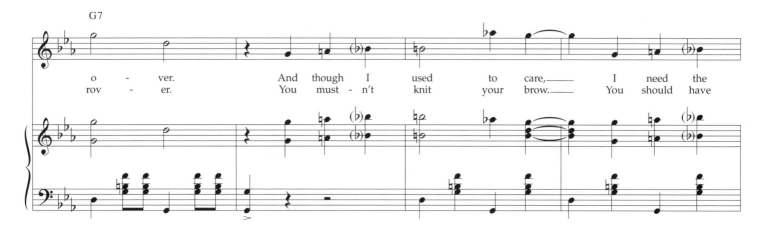

o - ver. And though I used to care,_____ I need the
rov - er. You must - n't knit your brow._____ You should have

gut   mein   Herr,_____   und   vor -   bei._____
fine   af -   fair,_____   but   now   it's   o -   ver.

Du   kennst   mich   wohl,   mein   Herr._____   Ach,   le - be
And   though   I   used   to   care,_____   I   need   the

wohl,   mein   Herr._____   Du   sollst   mich   nie   mehr   se - hen,   mein
o -   pen   air._____   You're   bet - ter

Herr.   Bye   bye   mein   off   with - out_____ me,   You'll

AND ALL THAT JAZZ

from CHICAGO

Words by FRED EBB
Music by JOHN KANDER

Moderately

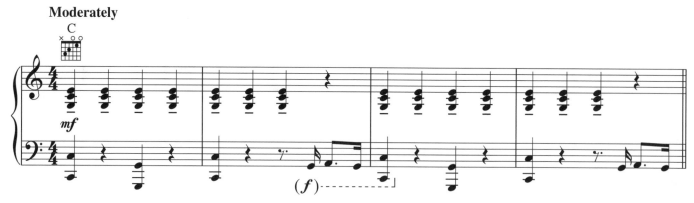

Come on, babe,_ why don't we paint the town,_ and all that jazz!_ I'm gon-na

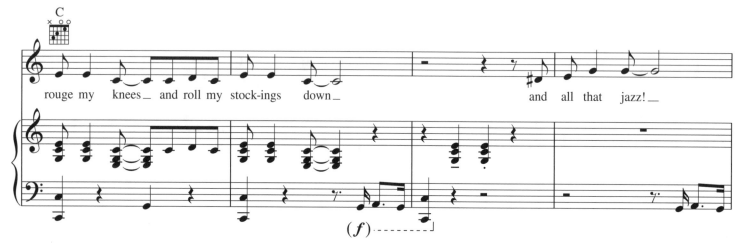

rouge my knees_ and roll my stock-ings down_ and all that jazz!_

Start the car,_ I know a whoop-ee spot_ where the gin is cold_ but the pi-an-o's hot._ It's just a

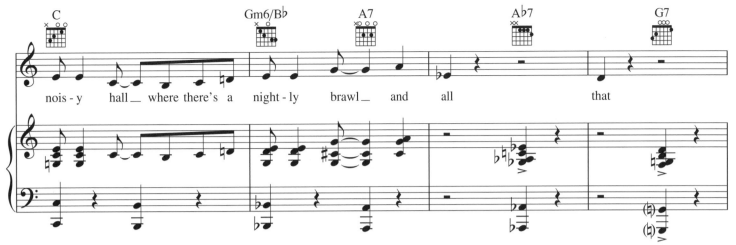

noi - sy hall __ where there's a night - ly brawl __ and all that

jazz! Slick your hair __ and wear your

buck - le shoes __ and all that jazz! __ I hear that Fa - ther Dip __ is gon - na

blow the blues __ and all that jazz! __ Hold on, hon, __ we're gon - na

bun - ny hug, __ I bought some as-pi - rin __ down at U - nit-ed Drug __ In case we shake a - part __ and want a

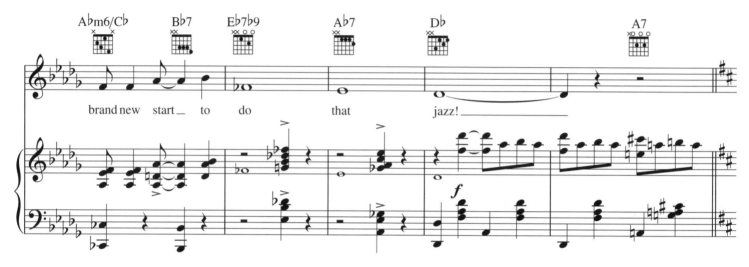

brand new start __ to do that jazz! _____

Oh, _____ I'm gon-na see my She - ba shim-my shake. __ (And all that jazz!)

Oh, _____ she's gon-na shim-my till her gar-ters break. __ (And all that jazz!) __ Show ____

Come on, babe,__ we're gon-na brush the sky.__ I bet-cha luck-y Lin - dy nev - er

all that jazz!__ Show _____ me where to park my gir - dle, Oh, _____

flew so high,__ 'Cause in the stra - to - sphere__ how could he lend an ear__ to all

__ my moth-er's blood-'d cur - dle if she'd hear__ her ba-by's queer__ for all

that jazz!

No, I'm no one's wife,_ but oh, I

love my life_ and all _____ that _____

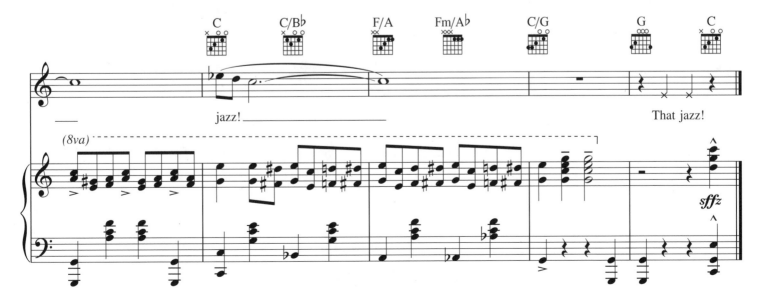

_____ jazz! _____ That jazz!

RAZZLE DAZZLE
from CHICAGO

Words by FRED EBB
Music by JOHN KANDER

183

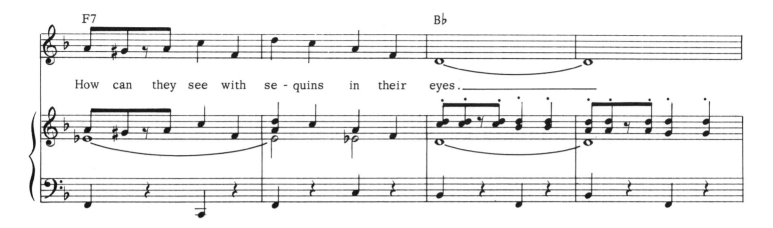

How can they see with se-quins in their eyes.

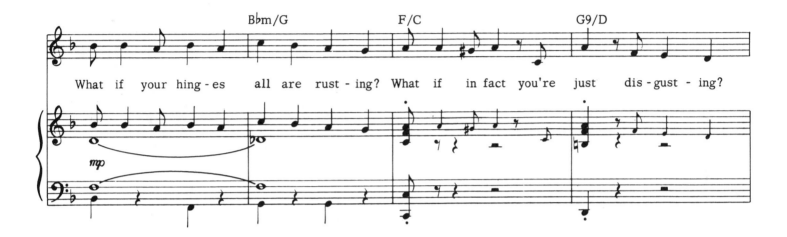

What if your hing-es all are rust-ing? What if in fact you're just dis-gust-ing?

Raz-zle daz-zle 'em and they'll nev-er catch wise

Give 'em the old raz-zle daz-zle.

Raz - zle daz - zle 'em. Give 'em a show that's so splen-dif - er-ous,

row af - ter row will grow vo-cif - er-ous. Give 'em the old flim flam flum-mox.

Fool and frac-ture 'em. How can they hear the truth a - bove the

roar._____ Throw 'em a fake and a fi - na - gle.

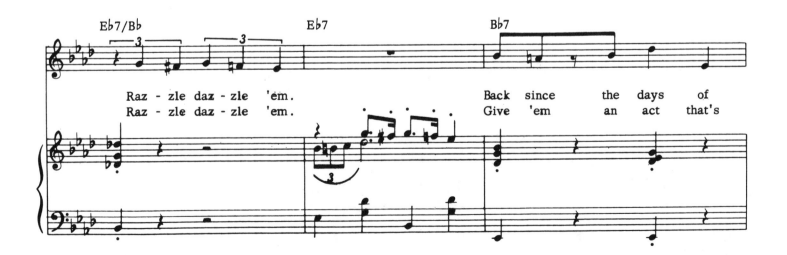

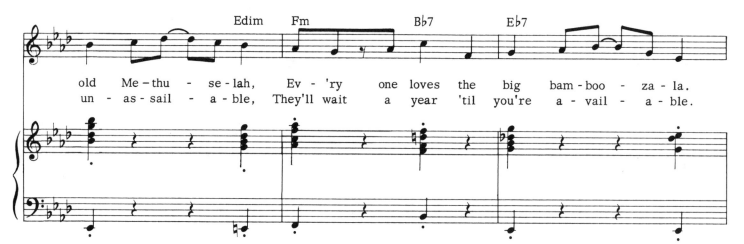

old Me–thu–se–lah, Ev–'ry one loves the big bam–boo–za–la.
un–as–sail–a–ble, They'll wait a year 'til you're a–vail–a–ble.

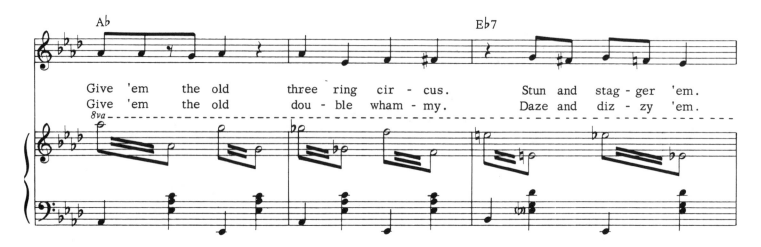

Give 'em the old three ring cir–cus. Stun and stag–ger 'em.
Give 'em the old dou–ble wham–my. Daze and diz–zy 'em.

When you're in trou–ble go in–to your dance.
Show 'em the first rate sor–cer–er you are.

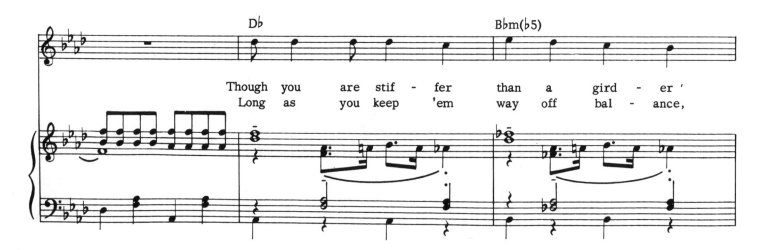

Though you are stif–fer than a gird–er '
Long as you keep 'em way off bal–ance,

BROADWAY BABY

from FOLLIES

Words and Music by
STEPHEN SONDHEIM

Broad-way Ba - by, _____ Learn-ing how to sing and dance, _

Wait-ing for that one big chance _ to be in a show. _____

Gee, I'd like to be _____ on some mar - quee, _____ All twin - kling lights, _ a

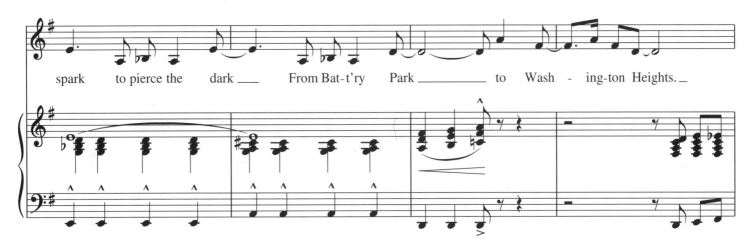

spark to pierce the dark ___ From Bat-t'ry Park _____ to Wash - ing-ton Heights. _

Some day, may-be, _____ All my dreams will be re - paid. _

_____ Hell, I'd e - ven play the maid _____ to be in a

show! _____ Say, Mis - ter Pro-duc - er, _____

I'm talk - ing to you, ___ sir. _____ I don't need a lot,

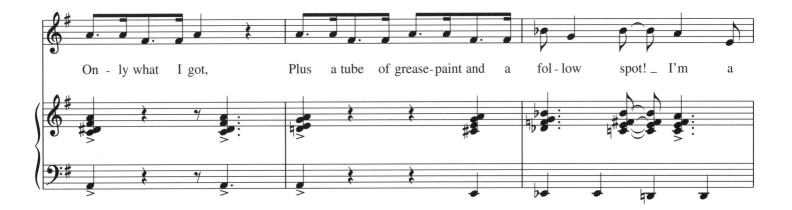

On - ly what I got, Plus a tube of grease-paint and a fol - low spot! I'm a

Broad - way Ba - by, _____ Slav - ing at a five and ten, _

_____ Dream - ing of the great day when _ I'll be in a

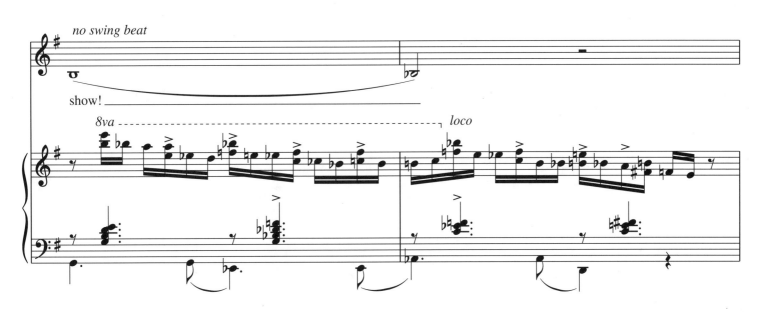

no swing beat

show! _____

Broad-way Ba - by, _____ Mak-ing rounds all af - ter - noon, _

Eat - ing at a greas-y spoon _ to save on my dough. _____

Solid 4

At my ti - ny flat ___ there's just my cat, _____ a bed _ and a chair. _

Still I'll stick it till ___ I'm on a bill _____ All o - ver Times Square. _

Some day, may - be, _____ If I stick it long e - nough, _

_ I can get to strut my _ stuff, _

cresc.

Work - ing for a nice man like a Zieg - feld or a Weiss - man in a great big

f

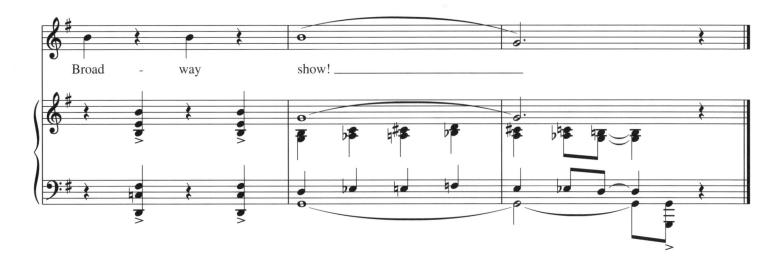

Broad - way show! _____

LOSING MY MIND
from FOLLIES

Words and Music by
STEPHEN SONDHEIM

Sempre molto rubato

mid-dle of the floor, Not go - ing left, Not go - ing right.

I dim __ the lights And think __ a - bout you, Spend sleep - less nights

To think __ a - bout you. You said __ you loved me, Or were you just be - ing kind? __

Or am I los - ing my mind?

rall.

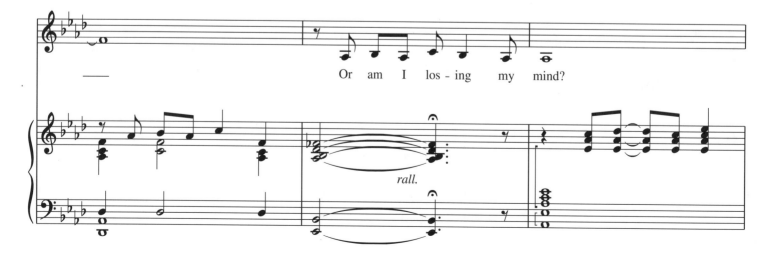

I want __ you so, It's like I'm los - ing my mind. __

Does no __ one know?

It's like I'm los-ing my mind.

accel.

Faster *(colla voce)*

All af-ter-noon, do-ing ev-'ry lit-tle chore, The thought of you stays

bright. Some-times I stand in the mid-dle of the floor,

Not go-ing left, Not go-ing right. I dim the lights

R.H.

And think _ a - bout you, Spend sleep - less nights To think _ a - bout

you, You said _ you loved me, _____ Or, were you just be-ing kind? _____

Or am I los - ing my _ mind? _____

COMEDY TONIGHT
from A FUNNY THING HAPPENED ON THE WAY TO THE FORUM

Words and Music by
STEPHEN SONDHEIM

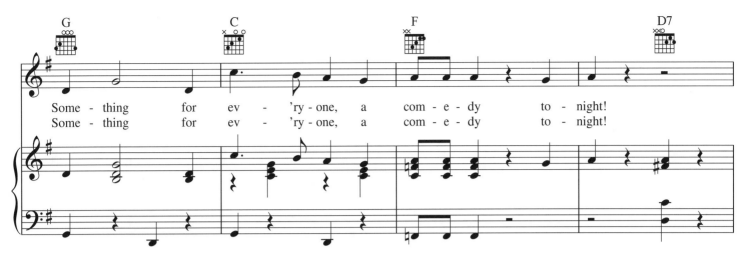

Some - thing for ev - 'ry - one, a com - e - dy to - night!
Some - thing for ev - 'ry - one, a com - e - dy to - night!

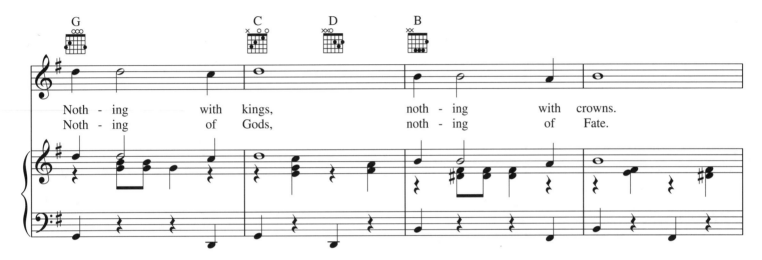

Noth - ing with kings, noth - ing with crowns.
Noth - ing of Gods, noth - ing of Fate.

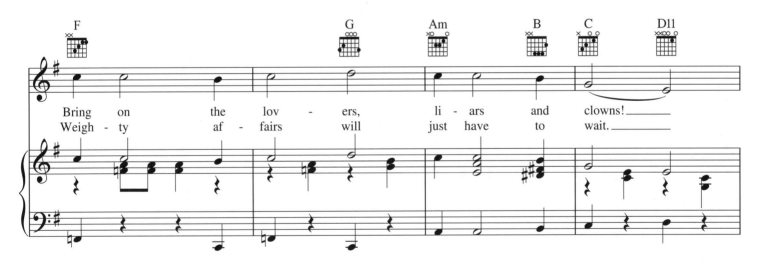

Bring on the lov - ers, li - ars and clowns!_____
Weigh - ty af - fairs will just have to wait._____

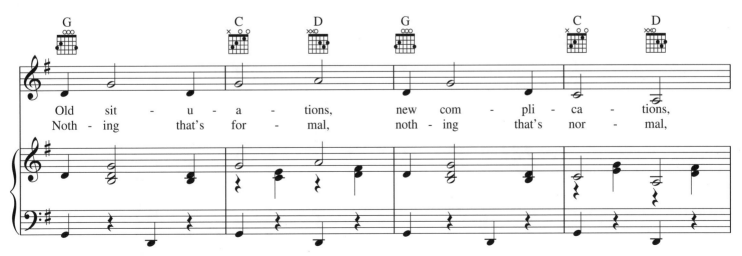

Old sit - u - a - tions, new com - pli - ca - tions,
Noth - ing that's for - mal, noth - ing that's nor - mal,

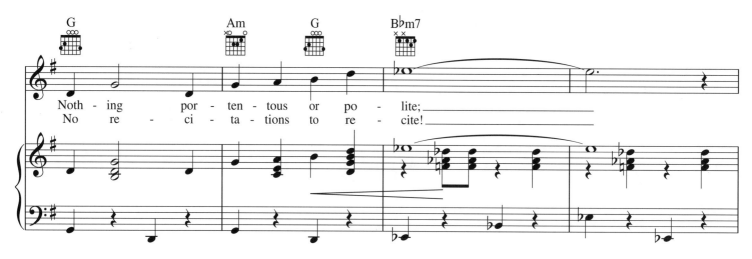

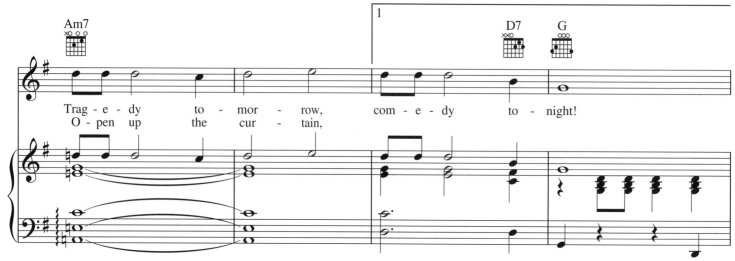

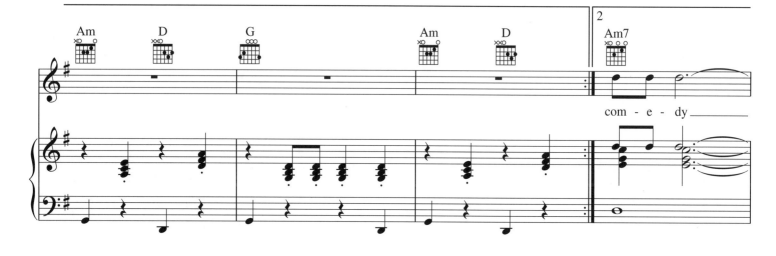

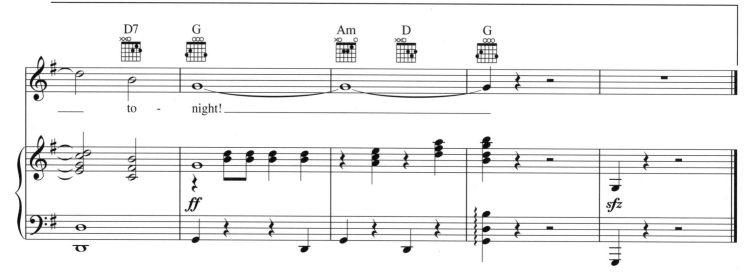

SO IN LOVE

from KISS ME, KATE

Words and Music by
COLE PORTER

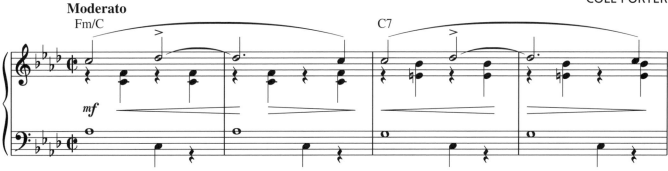

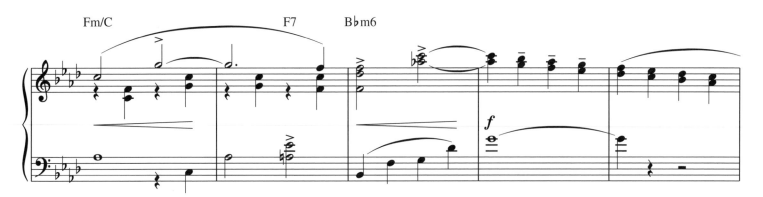

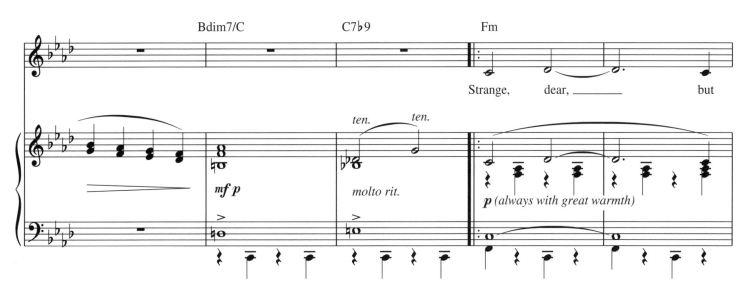

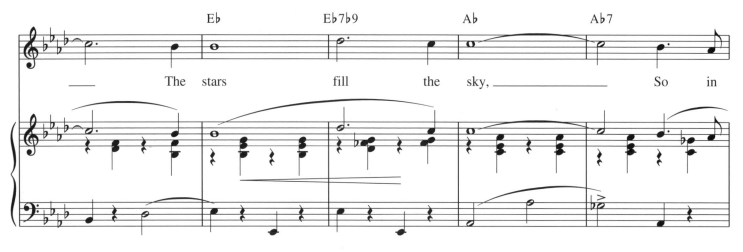

The stars fill the sky, _____ So in

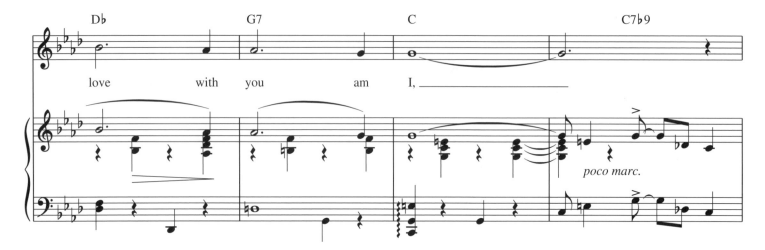

love with you am I, _____

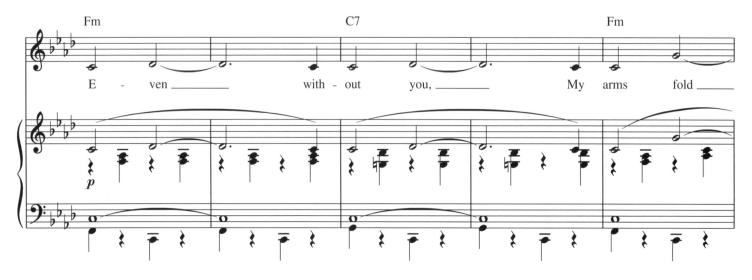

E - ven _____ with - out you, _____ My arms fold _____

_____ a - bout you, _____ You know, dar - ling,

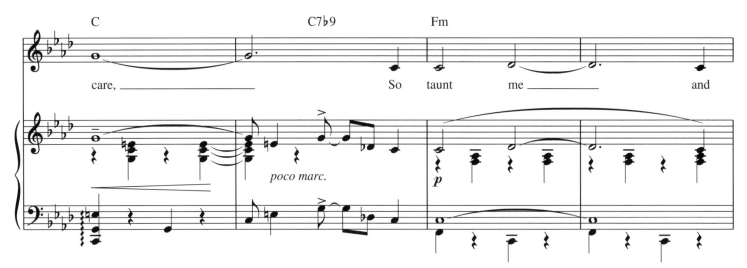

care, _____ So taunt me _____ and

hurt me, _____ De - ceive me, _____ De - sert me. _____

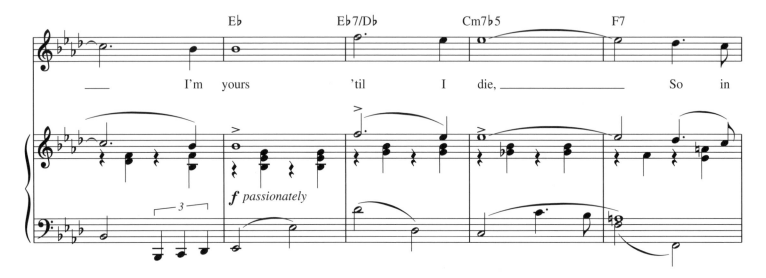

_____ I'm yours 'til I die, _____ So in

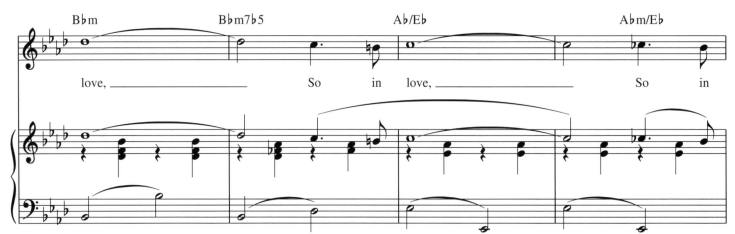

love, _____ So in love, _____ So in

love   with   you,   my   love _____   am

I.

I.

BRUSH UP YOUR SHAKESPEARE

from KISS ME, KATE

Words and Music by
COLE PORTER

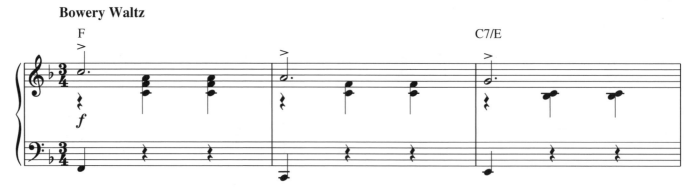

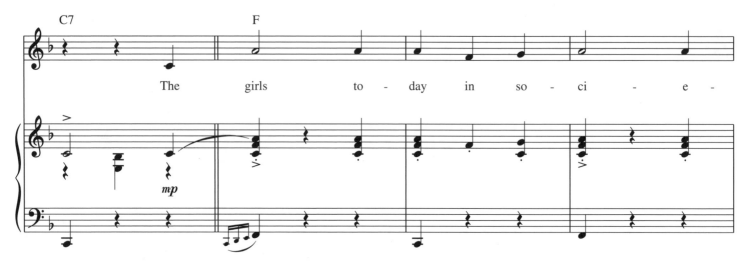

The girls to-day in so-ci-e-ty

ty Go for clas-si-cal po-et-

ry, So, to win their hearts, one must quote with

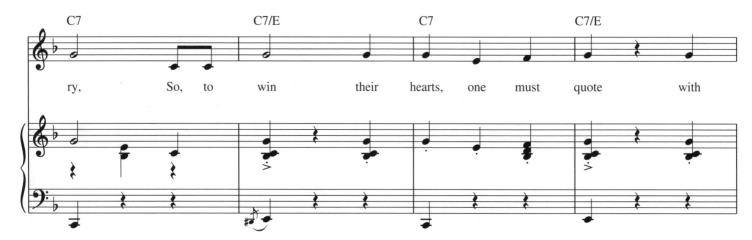

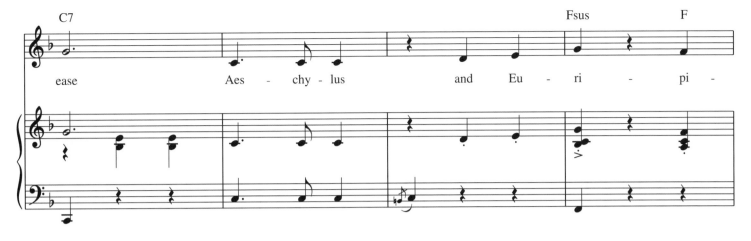

ease Aes - chy - lus and Eu - ri - pi -

des, One must know Ho - mer and b'lieve me,

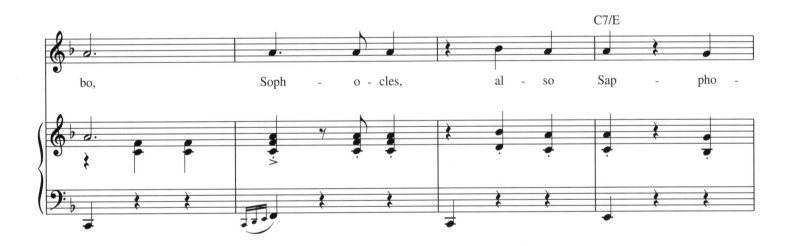

bo, Soph - o - cles, al - so Sap - pho -

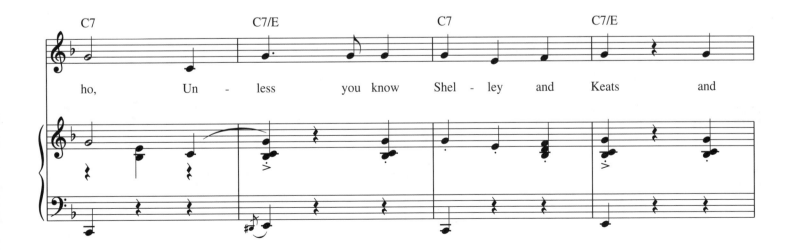

ho, Un - less you know Shel - ley and Keats and

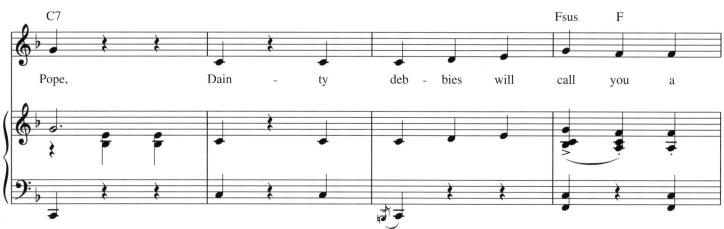

Pope, Dain - ty deb - bies will call you a

dope. But the po - et of them all _____

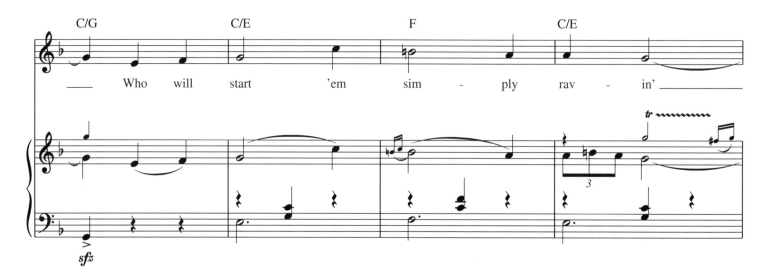

_____ Who will start 'em sim - ply rav - in' _____

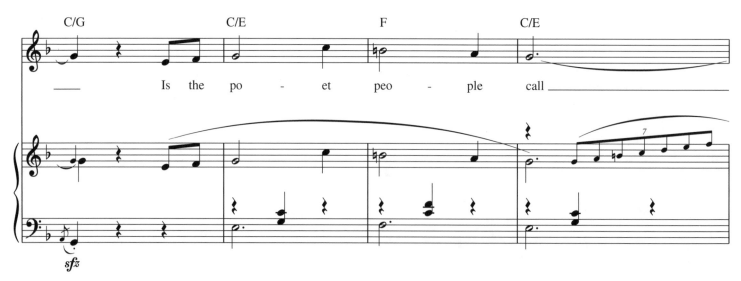

_____ Is the po - et peo - ple call _____

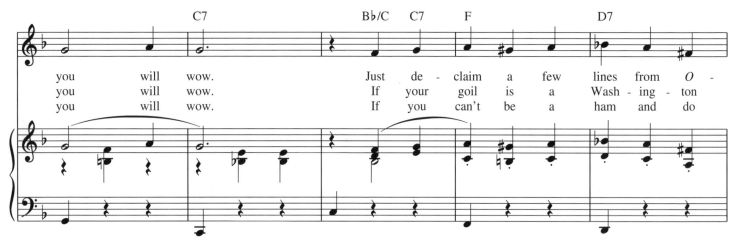

you will wow. Just de- claim a few lines from O-
you will wow. If your goil is a Wash- ing- ton
you will wow. If you can't be a ham and do

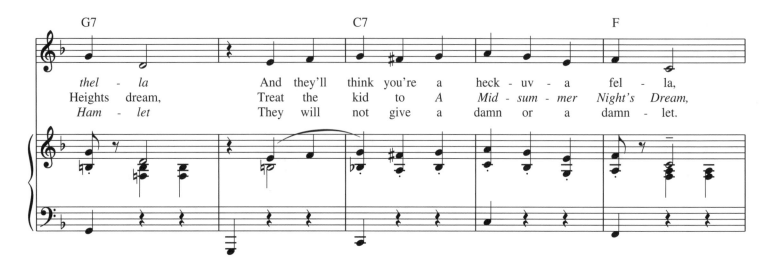

thel - *la* And they'll think you're a heck- uv- a fel- la,
Heights dream, Treat the kid to *A Mid* - *sum* - *mer Night's Dream,*
Ham - *let* They will not give a damn or a damn- let.

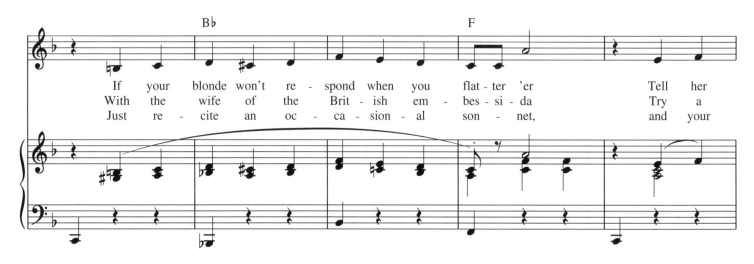

If your blonde won't re- spond when you flat- ter 'er Tell her
With the wife of the Brit- ish em- bes- si- da Try a
Just re- cite an oc- ca- sion- al son- net, and your

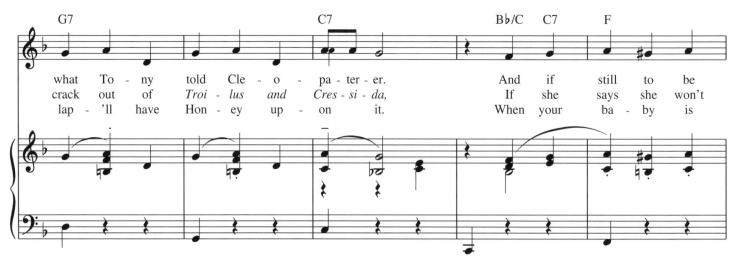

what To- ny told Cle- o- pa- ter- er. And if still to be
crack out of *Troi* - *lus and Cres* - *si* - *da,* If she says she won't
lap- 'll have Hon- ey up- on it. When your ba- by is

Lyrics (verse 1 / 2 / 3):

shocked she pre-tends, well, Just re-mind her that *All's Well That*
buy it or tike* it, Make her *tike it, what's more, *As You*
plead-ing for plea-sure Let her sam-ple your *Mea-sure for*

End's Well. Brush up your Shake-speare
Like It. Brush up your Shake-speare
Mea-sure. Brush up your Shake-speare

And they'll all kow - tow! _____
And they'll all kow - tow! _____
And they'll all kow -

[3] tow! _____

Cockney for "take"

SEVENTY SIX TROMBONES
from Meredith Willson's THE MUSIC MAN

By MEREDITH WILLSON

TILL THERE WAS YOU
from Meredith Willson's THE MUSIC MAN

By MEREDITH WILLSON

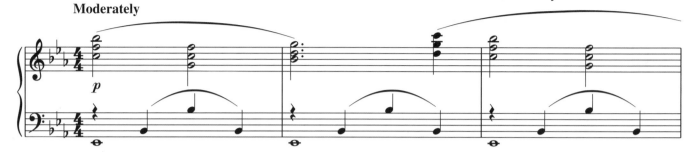

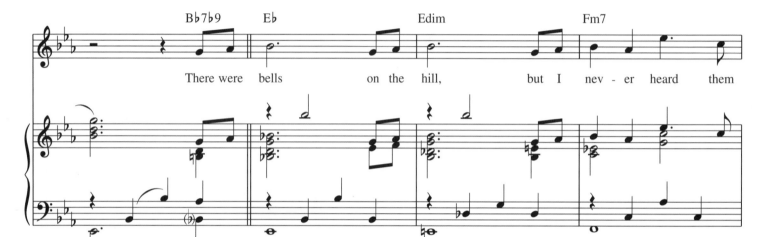

There were bells on the hill, but I nev-er heard them

ring-ing, No, I nev-er heard them at all till there was

you. _____ There were birds in the sky, but I

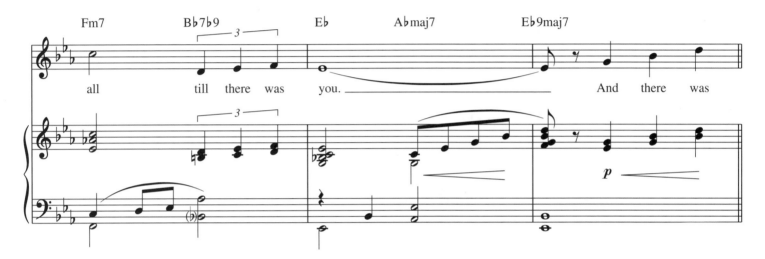

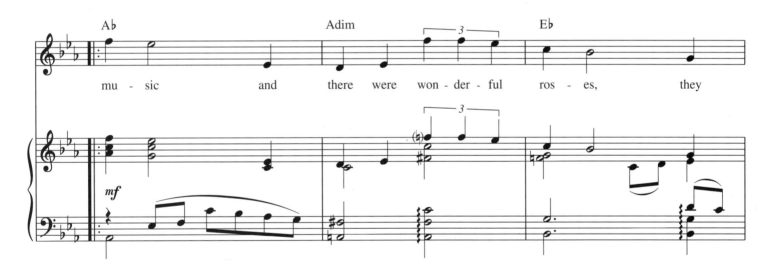

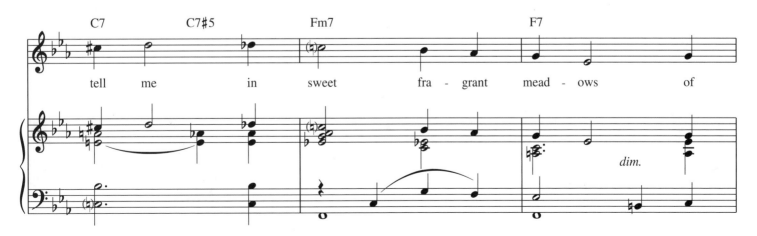

dawn, and dew, There was love all a-

round, but I nev - er heard it sing - ing, No, I

nev - er heard it at all till there was you.

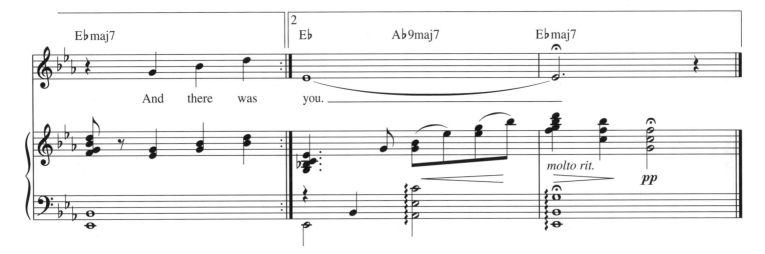

And there was you.

molto rit.

MY NEW PHILOSOPHY

from YOU'RE A GOOD MAN, CHARLIE BROWN

Words and Music by
ANDREW LIPPA

SALLY: *Spoken (before the vamp): "Why are you telling me?" (beat) I like it.*

* *Original key: A Major*

The song is a duet for Sally and Schroeder. The composer created this solo edition for publication.

Sal-ly Brown, _ your grades are go-ing down." _ I could have

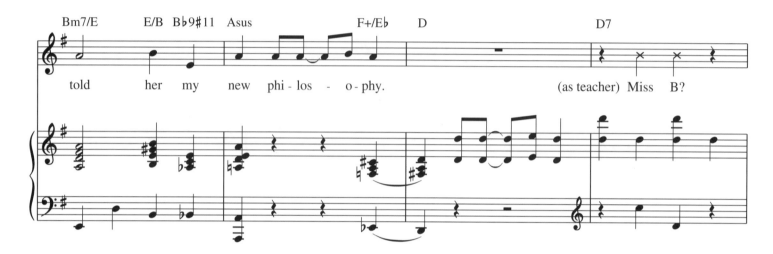

told her my new phi-los - o-phy. (as teacher) Miss B?

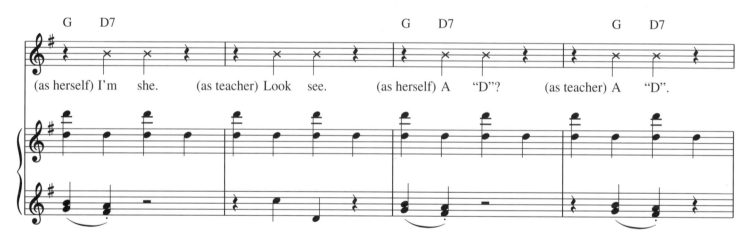

(as herself) I'm she. (as teacher) Look see. (as herself) A "D"? (as teacher) A "D".

Spoken (as herself): Well, why are you telling me? And that's my new phi - los - o - phy!! _

Spoken: Schroeder says, "Anything that takes only a minute can't be very lasting. For instance, Beethoven took over two years to complete his brilliant Ninth Symphony." (beat)

I can't stand it. (beat)
I can't stand it?
I like it!

VAMP

Stride-time!

De-cid - ing __ what goes in it. Some take a life-time, mine take a min - ute.

It's like a guar-an - tee, __ my new phi-los-o - phy, __ and things are sure to be __ a whole lot bright - er.

Spoken (trying out her new philosophies): Oh yeah,

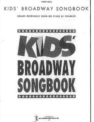